Own your life

ACHIEVE

PERSONAL EXCELLENCE

Keleapere Maggie Chalebgwa

Published by Horizon Designs & Printing
P.O. Box 403301 Gaborone
Tel: 0267 3947326

ISBN: 978-99912-940-0-1

Contents

Introduction

No one is ever truly happy turning out mediocre products. For most, we tend to be helpless to improve our situation. This book is about self-development, something that you will successfully achieve because you would have found the 'true you'. When you are aware what your strengths are, you are likely to play them up to advantage, and in the same way being aware of your weaknesses will allow you to decide what you avoid and what you work on improving. Personal excellence is about giving your very best, in the process developing essential skills that ensure your continued success as well as enjoying personal fulfilment.

We can all do something positive with our lives - each of us have it in us to succeed, yet only a few make it to the top. Most people find it difficult to move forward even with all years of experience at work or with family.

What most people need is to find themselves. Get a chance to know what really makes the individual tick.

What are the things that matter most to me?
What do I like doing?
What am I good at?
What do I expect my life to be like ten years from now?
How would I get to where I would like to be in the future? etc.

You begin to realise that your purpose in life is not as clear as you may have thought it was. In some cases you cannot spell out the special attributes that make you distinctly different from the next person; and it is difficult to define what your fears and hopes are. When such is true about you, you will find it difficult to work out a game plan for the future, you cannot confidently decide what is it that you are going to do to get the best out of your life. Such a situation will only reduce you to receiving instructions from your supervisor to get your job done; doing only what is expected both on the job and out of it, and generally relying on others to make decisions for you. A lifetime of this can only reduce you to a shadow of yourself, it will deny you the opportunity to experience the ultimate in achievement as you mainly do what is known and has been tested.

The ability to change and make the best of yourself lies within you. You must desperately want to do something worthwhile with your life, define that which you want in very clear terms to yourself and reflect on how best to make it come to pass if you are to make your mark. To do this you have to know yourself. You can start where you are now, as long as you realise that you are the sum total of your past. All the major successes and the small ones that you may think are insignificant, all the small and big mistakes you ever made, are a part of who you are today. All these are important in helping you look inside yourself to see what is important to you, your motivation and be able to clarify where you intend to be.

Try out the suggested activities and they will give you a chance to practice as needed.

Section I

Know Your Space

Take your position in life. Start with what you have. Your skills, education, employment, experience, knowledge, etc. are the bases on which anyone can start working towards achieving personal excellence.

"If a man hasn't discovered something that he will die for, he isn't fit to live".
Martin Luther King, Jr

1

Your self-worth

You are born to serve others - born for a purpose. And you grow in the direction of taking position in life. This is a must for us to get to do that which we have to do, the only way to fulfill your life purpose. Think about all the things you enjoy doing and those that you do because someone, a parent or coach, has told you to do. You may choose to stick with what you like best. They may be asking you to do something because 'it is the right thing to do' in their view. Doing what others ask you to do with the awareness that you need to have your own work designed by yourself is the right step in the direction of achieving personal excellence. In that way you are on your way to fulfilling your purpose.

You therefore have to get in touch with your inner self so that you understand who you really are. When you have an understanding of the purpose for your life, your values, attributes, fears and hopes you are likely to take charge of your own life. The knowledge you have will provide you the basis for the decisions you make and you could then focus on getting the best out of yourself. You will be better able to understand why you were able or unable to win on your set targets. You will be able to confidently acknowledge your strengths and take advantage of them, and by knowing your weaknesses you can play them down either by systematically working on improving on them or by avoiding them. Whatever you do, you build towards personal growth, gaining knowledge of self and the skills you will continue to need in the future. When you understand yourself, you will be better able to control your behaviour and its influence on the outcomes of the events in your life.

Reasonable thinking will determine that you consider your special attributes, your strengths and weaknesses, and use these as the basis for working towards your self worth. To get to grow and develop yourself to what you want to become and the best you can ever be, you have to be part of the creative process that will bring it to pass. At the same time be aware that you have to take responsibility and put the process in place. As part of the process you need to understand the effect you have on the events taking place around you, your interpretation of such events and the actions of those around you.

Reflecting on your reactions to what happens will be a good start as it will work on minimizing the effect of your denial, your blaming others for your circumstances and your placing the responsibility for your growth on them. Getting to understand what drives you, coming to terms with your limitations and making sense of what you intend to achieve will help you to make valid and reasonable decisions which do not fluctuate. Socrates once said, "Give me beauty in the inward soul; may the outward and the inward man be at one" It is those who understand themselves more than they understand others that can be called intelligent. Those who control others may consider themselves powerful, but it is the person who has mastered himself that is mightier.

With better knowledge of what motivates you, you are able to control your emotions and live a disciplined life in your own terms, as well as being in a position to contribute fully to the welfare of others. It is not only that you will have confidence and be able to provide answers to questions about yourself to others and self clearly and professionally, you will identify yourself as a leader or coach who is able to represent himself or herself fully in personal, prefessional and social lives identifying yourself from your own space, taking charge of your desire, wants, needs and values.

There are always two side to a coin, the one you are and the one you are not. When you drift along and not taking control of your life you will end up pushing yourself to do things that do not represent you well. This will always leave you unfulfilled. By using your skills and talents well you remain active and acquire experience that will work for you. There is no substitute for experience.You need to develop skills and acquire relevant knowledge in order to achieve personal excellence. It will put you in a position to make a distiction between taking charge of your life and drifting with the winds. To take charge of your life you have to start with what you have.
- Family - no one has ever been able to stand up without his/her background. So in any situation whenever one has to start with what they have, family is the first. Together, knowledge and skills form one side of the coin. These allow you to keep growing.
- Self-imposed limitations such as drifting along with some social groups will not benefit your personal development. Here you hardly grow.

Remember, the choices you make on daily basis are influenced by whether you intend to be proactive and be the driver in your life or you take the back sit and let life happen to you.

As you take stock of your inner self, seek to come to terms with what you really have in there that makes your life worthy. Allow yourself to be curious about what you can do and what you were meant to become. Whatever you engage in, be passionate about it; give it your best. All this will push you higher, getting rid of uncertainties that often come with lack of awareness of one's abilities and failing to take advantage of opportunities. Your worth is the sum total of accumulated skills, knowledge and experiences. Step forward and claim your life place, that which you can get only by utilizing your special gifts.

> ==> To claim your life you have to put your true self out there and make it work for you.
> ==> Having confidence in your personal worth makes it possible for you to move forward and do the best that you have to do.

2

Your experiences

Most people are comfortable doing the same things daily with little variation. Although the routine of it makes them comfortable because there will be few surprises and shocks that may upset them, it also means that one is unlikely to experience new excitements and the range of skills gained is limited. There will be few hard decisions to make and they will grow to do what they do without thinking. By following your routine, you hardly face the need to make choices demanding dropping one option or the other. After some years you may come to realize that you only know limited stuff. You only know what is in the range of your exposure.

You are the sum total of all the things that happened to you, your past achievements, the choices you made and what you expected to become by it all. You are a product of your joys and sorrows, your likes and dislikes, successes and failures, your strengths and handicaps, influences from family, friends and even your geographical location. You may or may not have played an active part in what you have become, you nevertheless could have easily been a different person to what you are today if you were exposed to a different set of experiences. Just by making different choices to those you made in the past, choosing different friends, having different dreams and expectations from life, you could have become something different to what you are now. All the choices you made in the past have produced the person you are today.

Take time to think about your past so that you get to realize that what you are now is not just a matter of chance. It is a product of a lifetime of choices. We all have inner voices which when we attentively listen to we can hear telling us what to do. They are the reason we sometimes hesitate when we were meant to attempt new things. We at times hear a voice of doubt that may tell us 'no you cannot do this or that'. All of these may be coming from a place inside of you that tells you that there is something about you that is not visible to others. You always have a moment when you briefly reflect on what you are about to do and possible consequences for your life.

Get in touch with both your positive and negative feelings about events in your life. Identify significant events in your life in chronological order and how they related to your state of wellbeing. For each, search your memory so that you get to re-live the feelings that accompanied it at the time.

- Allow yourself to engage in an internal dialogue with the protagonists (or your internal characters who advised you) and listen to their responses to those events of the distant past.
- Note the decisions that you took then, feel the attitude under which they were taken – was it fear, anger, excitement or pleasure? Would you have made the same decisions today or would you change some aspects of them?

By going through this, you will make clear to yourself where you are coming from. You outline your personal history by clarifying the historical antecedents relative to the aspects of the life you are exploring.

Choices I made	What motivated my choices	Choices that I would repeat

From the above exercise you will be able to get to understand where you are coming from, your past and how it has made you what you are today. Some of the events will be painful to you even if they could have been pleasing to others. Some would have directly pleased you. Whichever state an event has evoked, allow yourself to feel it so that you decide how it has affected the turn of events in your life. You should be able to identify those events that have made a positive contribution to your personality and those that have had a negative effect. Be sure to expound on your answer so that you become aware of the reasons you hold for how your choices have contributed to your present situation.

How have the decisions you made in the past affected your life in the areas of:
- Relationship with family members?
- Education? How well you applied yourself to school work?
- Career choice? Why did you choose your career?

Choices I made	Nature of contribution (positive/negative)

Acknowledging the negative experiences you have had in your life will help you work out that which you would like to see changed so that you get to achieve your life purpose. In this way you clarify to self where you are going with your life. It also makes active the positive points that will amplify your potential, illuminate your direction and destination in life, help define your goals and establish your guiding vision. You also become aware of what is stopping you from achieving your life purpose, the constraints, the blocks and obstacles that hinder your progress toward your goals. The positive effects will clarify what you need to concentrate on and tap on to continue to achieve your life purpose.

Reflection

- Are there choices you made in the past that you now wish you had not made?
- Make a list of such choices and start making a plan how you will change them, and show what their effect in the future will be.

3

Your Strength

All the things that are important to us are our values. Values are the broad preferences that affect the course of action one takes or the outcomes of our actions. They reflect one's sense of right and wrong or what 'aught' to happen. The feelings you have with respect to arising events reflect your values. The extent of your outrage with respect to an event or issue under consideration may surprise those who hold an opinion and values different to yours. It is important to realize that values differ for different people and influence their behavior and reactions. In the same way therefore be aware of your values and understand why you do things the way you do.

How we come by our values is a complex process deeply rooted at our very core, and as such values are very difficult to change. Most of us learned our values or morals at home, at church, mosque or synagogue, at school. Personal values provide an internal reference for what is good, important, useful, constructive, beneficial, etc. It is from such reference points that we behave in ways others see and would judge us.

Our values are our source of strength. They give us an image of what we are aiming at and will motivate our actions as we put our energy into achieving that which we consider important. Through your understanding what your strengths are in getting what you believe in you make focused choices and avoid unpleasantness and weak points as needed. Understanding your values helps anticipate likely problems on the way to achieving one's goal; it creates interest and enthusiasm to keep going on.

Clarify your values

Since values are traits that define what you consider worthwhile, they represent your highest priorities and deeply held driving forces. You bring values to any work you deal with; as such others would judge you on the basis of choices you make and your style of doing things. Take time to reflect on principles which guide you when you:
- make decisions concerning people you live and work with.
- judge other people's actions.
- make choices about things you have to do.

Whatever the answers you come up with, it will give you an idea about those guiding principles you use as a measure for what happens in your life and around you. You are guided by what you consider important, i.e. your values and these become the basis for the judgments you make.

A list of some values, presented in alphabetical order, is given on the next page. Although they may all seem good, some will mean more to you than others. Carefully go through the list and rank in order the ten values you endorse most strongly, with the one at the top representing the most important or the value that matters most to you:

Achievement - being accomplished
Advancement - promotion
Athletic excellence
Career success
Competitiveness - winning, willingness to take risks
Conformity
Creativity - innovativeness
Discipline
Diversity
Gaining recognition - status
Giving and compassion for others
Good health
Helpfulness - contributing to improving society
Influence over others
Independence / autonomy
Inner harmony - being at peace with yourself
Integrity - honesty in all dealings
Involvement - belonging to a group
Knowing the right people
Knowledge - wisdom
Loyalty - obedience / respectfulness
Mentoring others
Orderly home life
Open-mindedness
Personal development
Pleasure - fun, leisurely life-style
Projecting the right image
Self-respect - sense of personal identity
Self-sufficiency
Serving others
Stability
Trusting and serving God
Understanding other cultures
Wealth - getting rich

Write out your 10 highest scoring or most important values.

Values in order of priority

1.	6.
2.	7.
3.	8.
4.	9.
5.	10.

Carefully study your top 10 values and determine:
1. Which values are being relatively satisfied at present, and which values are not satisfied.
2. How is your life affected by each of the 10 values?
3. Suggest ways you could change your situation to get to satisfy your values. Discuss your answers with a friend or trusted family member.
4. In what ways are your values contributing to your accomplishing what you consider to be your life purpose?

Some of the values are not an end unto themselves. For instance, although you may value wealth, it may be just a means through which you get to fulfill some other values. Wealth may allow you to pursue leisurely lifestyle or may make you feel secure. So, as you pursue such a value do not lose sight of what may really be the reason you drive yourself so hard. Set time aside to play, enjoy your wealth with family and friends, for that may well be the most important value to you where money only provides the opportunity to do it right.

Acquiring the highest qualification possible may seem

important. Yet, the reality of your situation may be getting a career that will be most fulfilling. The qualifications just provide you the opportunity to be considered for relevant jobs. This is also true for feeling the need to score high marks in class. You need to figure out if these marks are accompanied by the right skills that will enable you to be effective in your chosen field of work in the future.

Shaping of values

The environment we grow in, that is, both family and friends we surround ourselves with, the school and workplace, religious or cultural beliefs and personal experiences as well as mass media influence are the main sources of the values we hold. As such it is parents, teachers and religious leaders who influence the values we end up with. With the present life styles our values are also influence by the media through television and Internet as well as children being affected by what they get from the streets.

The Role of Family

We acquire our values from a very young age as our families, then our friends or community first influence us. From them we learn what is right and wrong, desirable and undesirable. When what you do is unacceptable you get chastised or punished, and where you behave as expected you get rewarded in one way or the other. It is the way the punishment-reward technique is applied on us that we learn to stay with some actions, avoid some or even alter our behavior in order to conform to the expectations of those who influence us. The do's and don'ts we grow up with around the home reflect the values our parents hold. We eventually repeat these with our children if we believe in their 'correctness', or we even reject some.

Religious & cultural beliefs

Religious and cultural beliefs also affect us in similar ways, as does family. They tend to point out the right and wrong and prepare us for a future life. These beliefs will blend with values acquired from close family and relatives and become part of our upbringing. We use these values to solve common human problems for our survival and for learning to live together as a community.

Our friends, Schools we attend and the workplace

Every school has its own culture and it carries with it values that influence learners, and such will affect them for life. School values will touch on areas like the kind of citizen the school would like to produce, contribution to society now and in the future, positive contribution to high caliber members of the work force and specifically the quality of education provided. School values will merge with the values you bring from home, and those values you acquire or reinforce as you relate to your friends from childhood to adulthood. Our friends influence us such that we either accept some of their values, or modify our values to accommodate them, or be the reason the friends change their values to fit in with ours, - the case of peer influence. You will carry all the acquired values to the workplace where you pick new values and even continue to modify what you brought with you. Your values will continue to change as you go through different phases of adulthood.

The role of media

Our media heroes also play an important role in molding our values - you may admire your hero's accomplishments and their beliefs and choose to adopt them as your own. Your chosen hero becomes your role model and you would value that which you think has made them so successful and seem important to them.

Experience is a good teacher

Values come to us through experience too. Experience teaches one to either pursue or abandon a value. If what you experience does not bring you satisfaction and joy, you will move away from the source of discomfort. Where what you do and the rewards you get from it satisfy you, you will get to hold what you do in high esteem and live up to it.

We use our values to shape our purpose in life, and as such our goals will reflect our cherished values. However, our values will change as soon as our goals or life purpose changes. For instance, as soon as one becomes a parent there tends to be a shift in focus. Where one had been content to drift through life, getting as much fun as possible, a sense of responsibility will set in. You may now consider the values of security and stability to be vital and will engage in activities that will achieve these. The same might happen when you change from being an ordinary employee to a supervisor. There will be a shift in expectations and emphasis on values.

Every time a value is born, our lives take on a new meaning, and every time a value dies, some part of that meaning is lost forever. Choose well how you redirect your life. When you pick new values that uplift you, you fulfill you intention. It is sad when someone goes against their better judgment and successfully pursue a way of life that leaves them wanting. No matter what you achieve, you remain unfulfilled because the compromise made has taken you away from what you value.

It is those who ever dared believe that something inside of them was superior to circumstance that get to achieve something splendid. These are the people who do not settle for what they find themselves with but continue to question it. Those who give in to circumstance will only do very little. Where your values as they stand do not work for you, then you have to do something about them. In the long run, your values are your strength.

Reflection

- In what ways have your different friends influenced your choice of values?
- In what ways have the values espoused by your school affected your life?
- In what ways were your most important values influenced by family, friends, school values and religious or cultural beliefs?
- How has media contributed to the shaping of values in your generation?

How valuable are your values to you?

Are the things that you hold as important getting the best out of you? Do they bring the fulfillment you are looking for? For instance, if you value knowing the right people, you will need to know how to take advantage of this to make such an opportunity contribute toward improvements in your life. The important thing, in the long term, may not be that you control people. It would be what you get out of it when you do. If you value influence over others, there is a need to look into how well informed you are about what you influence them on. As such, do you maybe also value integrity and helpfulness? It is not just about having a value, but how valuable it is in your life and how valuable the supporting values are to ensure completeness in your life.

Your belief system can liberate or forever hold you prisoner. Where your values leave you envying other people who seem to be moving on, or leave you less confident of what you are working on, it is time to re-visit them to work out what to throw away, what you need to pick to support what you love to do or to be and even take on what you never considered before if it will help you better fulfill your life.

The meanings we attach to events as they unfold shape our lives. The bases and criteria for interpreting any events are our values. So, it is your values that determine the amount of effort you put in making a success of your life. In essence, these deeply held beliefs provide a guide as to where we apply our energies. Otherwise we are likely to run in all directions, doing anything and all things that come our way. Values give us direction. They guide us to our destination. And for you to enjoy the journey, your values have to be consistent and supportive of each other. Remember that you can and should shape your own future. Because if you do not, someone else will do that for you and you may not like the result.

Ensuring that your life gets attuned to your values will bring you inner peace, help you release the vital energy you need to get work done, make you enthusiastic and better able to fulfill your life purpose. Your behavior and your performance are greatly influenced by your preferences or expectations. The activities you engage in will give you skills and help you build competencies. Your strength will build and bring out the essential effectiveness that will make your life meaningful.

==> Being aware of what your values are will go a long way in helping you understand your behavior, disappointments as well as frustrations and anger whenever you think your values are compromised.

==> When you understand and live by your values, you gain control over your life. It helps you experience a sense of inner peace and total congruency that communicates a feeling that you are in control, and you are doing the right things right.

==> Your strength and confidence come through being able to stay with your values and having them work for you.

==> Your values affect the direction your life takes.

==> With your values well focused and working for you, you are well on your way to occupy your rightful space in the bigger scheme of things in life.

4

Your Life Purpose

The all-driving reason for our lives, our purpose, determines what we choose to do and how we choose to live our lives. Purpose embodies all the things you believe in that give meaning to why you live. It is what you look up to as the expected end result or what you set out to achieve. As you work your way to that predetermined goal, your values will affect and influence how you go about it, how you react to any problems and challenges you face and the decisions you make all the way. So it is your purpose and values that greatly determine how you set out to deal with issues and your reactions to them. Byknowing your purpose, you will be able to clearly define what you want to achieve and the decisions you make will be consistently directed toward helping you move towards its fulfillment. "There is one quality that one must possess to win, and that is definiteness of purpose, the knowledge of what one wants and a burning desire to achieve it." Napoleon Hill

To clarify for yourself what your purpose is, you need to understand what it is that you want to achieve - that which you are looking for and has the power to bring personal satisfaction. There is a possibility that what you feel is important to do and your chosen career is not concomitant.

For instance, you may strongly feel it is important to spend your days using your music talent and creative skills as an artist to raise awareness of the plight of the less privileged. Yet, you were trained as an accountant and now you make your living working in a high-powered organization as head of accounts. Come to terms with your emotions so that what you feel and what you want are consistent. Your experiences, your strengths and the decisions you made in the past are part of what you pay attention to when you clarify your purpose. You may need to venture out to pursue your passion and use your career experience to manage what you do. When you have resolved the incongruence, you will experience a special energy that resonates with you deeply.

Reflection:

- What is it that you want to achieve with your life?
- Make a list of all the things you want to achieve in those areas of your life you consider important. e.g. your family, your career and vocation, health, education, talents, fulfilling childhood dreams and ambitions, etc.
- Set yourself a deadline when you will achieve what you have set out for yourself.
- Is what you do with your life now consistent with that picture of what you want for yourself?
- What really is your life purpose?

What you consider important you tend to adopt as your purpose in life. It becomes something you do since it matters to you. Often the different areas of your life will assume importance at different times. This affects what you focus on at a given time.

Clarify your priorities

To get to what your life purpose is, you have to take into account where you are now. You have to be aware of the state of your affairs and where it is all leading to now. In some cases you could be drifting along and doing nothing to improve on your life, and you have to decide if you need to do something about it. Once you actively think about it, you would be able to decide what needs to be changed, improved or even left in place. For each area of your life you have to work out whether you are active or inactive, the extent to which you are satisfied or dissatisfied with it and if you need to change it in any way. The balance that you create in all the areas of your life will contribute to your overall success.

Table 4.1 has identified some areas that you could be concerned about now. You can add more to the list, then tick on an appropriate column for each area. Add as many of these areas as you are currently concerned about. Where the list seems to be too long, you will later on think about prioritizing the items.

Area of Life	Active	inactive	satisfied	dis-satisfied	To be changed
Family					
Career / vocation					
Education					
Health					

Table 4.1

You will find that you are at different levels of development for the different areas of your life. You are unlikely to focus

on all the items on your list at the same time or with the
same intensity. List those things you are dissatisfied with
and inactive in but would like to do. Keep thinking about
them as you read on.

Once you are satisfied that the table is as complete as
could be for now, you have to determine how attending to
the areas you are satisfied with makes it possible for you
to concentrate on achieving you purpose, and how what
you are dissatisfied with can affect you if you attend to it,
change it or even ignore it.

Establishing own priorities

Divide the information you have come up with and fit it
in the tables like those shown below showing areas of life
where you are actively building and are satisfied, active
but dissatisfied; inactive but satisfied, and inactive and
dissatisfied.

Active and satisfied with	Active but dissatisfied with

Inactive but satisfied with	Inactive and dissatisfied with

Reflection:

1. Active and satisfied with: you spend time and energy in
   this area and you say you are satisfied with how things
   are working out. You now have to consider if what you
   are satisfied with brings you joy; that when you have
   achieved in this area you do not feel a void, a craving

that you still have to look for something that will make you fulfilled. If you are still looking for fulfillment despite being satisfied with what you do then you are spending energy on something you have to consider changing.

2. ***Active but dissatisfied with:*** you may be doing things because others around you expect you to but your passion lies elsewhere. Be clear why you do this and note if it is worth pursuing. Draw inside yourself and determine what will happen if you were to drop what you are doing now and replace it with something that will fulfill you.

    Make a list of things you are actively doing but dissatisfied with and against each note why you are dissatisfied and how attending to it will change you.

3. ***Inactive but satisfied with:*** you are most probably sitting back and allowing things to happen to and for you. You are not applying yourself to achieve and bring satisfaction through your own effort. Your talents are not used, you are not allowing yourself to gain experience in the areas of life that will ensure your growth, and you may be barely contributing to solutions for problems around you. Inform yourself on why things happen and satisfy you – are others toiling on your behalf? Are you allowing yourself to be a parasite and fail to develop your talents, gain essential skills and experiences?

4. ***Inactive and dissatisfied with:*** you may be ignoring those areas of your life that you are passionate about. Your values and strengths may not be suitably aligned such that you are merely surviving and you need to attend to what you are dissatisfied with and find what will bring you joy. Make a list of things you are not doing anything about and you are dissatisfied with and against each note why you are dissatisfied and how attending to it will change you. If there is something preventing you from 'actively doing' decide how you will overcome this to attend what is important to you.

Establishing what your true purpose in life is is not easy, but the most difficult part is being able to focus your energies on working to become that purpose.

The things that bring satisfaction to you are essential to do – they are most likely to be in line to contributing to your achieving your true purpose. Whatever you do but leaves you wanting should alert you that there is something else you are not doing that you have to attend to. By prioritizing your activities it allows you to think about each one of them, visualize the consequences for doing it or not doing it, and therefore focus on what is of benefit to you. Over time you learn to concentrate on important and necessary tasks. When your priorities are clear to you, you may notice that it is the items that bring you satisfaction that you find important and you tend to enjoy doing.

Your purpose is the basis of your vision

When you have purpose you have true meaning for your life. It will enable you to create a picture of what the future will be like when your purpose is fulfilled. What you see in the future, your vision, will influence all your daily actions as you work on making it come to pass. Your vision acts as a Beacon, towards which you direct all actions that are intended to achieve your purpose.

Mentally put yourself in the future and look around to observe what you have in your life at that point in time. To do this, you have to think about what you would like to have in your life by that time. Draw a picture of what would be there for you. Generate clear conditions of satisfaction, that is, tangible evidence that you have achieved the elements of your vision. Complete table 4.2 below by adding on what you would like to have in the future, and describe how you

will know when you have it in place. The picture you draw
will be the visual representation of what you intend and
might even be easier to visualize than what you write.

What do I want?	How would I know I've got it?
A successful business	Have 125 employees; i.e. I am contributing to 125 people make a living/ improve their lives, etc.

Security - house
    - car
    - income
    - savings	

Table 4.2

Once you know what you would like to have in the future,
you will have to think of what you have to put in place
now, that which will help you achieve your goal. For
instance: What kind of business would you like that will
justify the 125 employees? What are you doing to prepare
for it? Details of what you do to prepare for the business
will include a plan of activities that will take you to your
destination. Your plan of action should include timelines for
the various activities you intend to engage in. In chapter 5
you will assess your motivators and this will further help
you plan your activities, and taking advantage of your
interests.

The future does not arrive overnight. We get to it one day
at a time. And, whatever you achieve in each day can either

take you closer to your envisioned future or farther from it. It is the activities that you concentrate on that contribute toward the realization of your vision.

Reflection:

- Write down what you expect your life to be like five years, ten years, twenty years from now.
- Are your actions focused on helping you achieve your purpose?
- Describe four points of action that support your effort to achieve your desired future.

==> Have a purpose for your life; then it will be exciting to wake up everyday to accomplish important objectives.

==> Know what your priorities are in all areas of your life. You will then focus on those areas that if fulfilled will bring you great satisfaction.

==> Visually enjoy your future life; then work on making that future a reality.

5

What gives you momentum?

Many good ideas have never been followed up and developed to fruition. They have remained as just wishful thinking. Generally, only a few people ever follow up on their ideas and can be seen working day and night to turn them into desired product. What might be the difference between these two groups of people? The answer may lie with what drives each of them, the motivation that determines how far they will go to get what they want. Some people seem content to have only the basics that ensure survival while others will never rest before they reach the highest possible in their career path. These people are differently driven. Their form of and levels of motivation are completely different.

Motivation refers to the 'inner urge' or passion, which constantly incites you to act in a particular way. It is this inner urge of your feelings and emotions, instincts and ingrained habits that give you the go-power that puts you into action. All the accompanying action is intended to meet the need to accomplish the consciously and unconsciously set goals or desires. This will satisfy your purpose and values as you strive to achieve personal fulfilment. It is mainly motivation that gives intensity and persistence of behavior that makes it possible to achieve one's purpose. Motivation gives reason for one to want to accomplish. If you have a big enough reason to want something, then you will create opportunities that will bring you closer and closer to its realisation. The reason you have compels you to behave the way you do.

Motivators

Different people are motivated for different reasons and no two people may equally share such a drive. It remains important that you take time to reflect and answer for yourself the question, 'What motivates me to do certain things or act in certain ways?' We can now look at some of the reasons people are motivated to act and accomplish their dreams. It could be any or many of the following, and none is any more important than others. If it is your reason and motivator, and it works for you, then it is important.

ADVENTURE: This is for people who enjoy creating new ways of doing things or coming up with new products. These are people who are not totally comfortable when they are expected to deal with the known and tested ways. They prefer to undertake activities where there is more than one possible answer. They gain satisfaction from testing their creativity. As a student you will do well in projects that allow you to freely test new ideas without being limited by an authority figure.

Being employed can at times allow the adventure-loving people to safely try out new ideas, tapping into the experience of their supervisors and colleagues. Such people will do well where their supervisors are prepared to support them, the managers who are forward looking and are not just content with maintaining the status quo. Otherwise they could find themselves frustrated and limited by the system they work in.

At another level there are those who prefer to be independent of others. They want to decide what to do and not follow other people's instructions. This may be difficult to totally achieve if somebody else employs you. Your employer's mission and vision will limit you, and as such you may have to seek alternative route to being independent. It thus becomes important to decide on the right career path where you will be better fulfilled.

Blindly following other people's dreams is limiting and leaves adventure lovers dissatisfied.

RECOGNITION: This goes well with the need to feel that you are worth something. Others notice your contribution and they make it known to you that it has made a difference to someone. The recognition received is more of a validation of one's worthiness, acknowledging that they are useful. The person's self-esteem is satisfied and this leads to feelings of increased self-worth, capability and adequacy. Recognising people for any accomplishments often acts as one of the best motivators in organizations. Such people will be driven to accomplish organizational goals as long as they realize their contribution is valued and they receive recognition that goes with it.

Some people may be seeking to be recognized for being knowledgeable in their chosen field. They get satisfaction in providing expert service. If they feel adequately recognised they will continue to research about their field and get to create opportunity to work and share their gained knowledge.

Those who seek material rewards and feel adequately compensated will also be willing to work hard for such recognition. Status symbols such as a company car and special allowances would be well accepted.

There are also those people whose actions are aimed at bringing about results that are recognizable and will earn them the respect of the community. They look forward to being counted amongst the great.

BENEVOLENCE: This may show itself in two ways. First, as a way of satisfying curiosity. This involves doing what is considered to be valuable for its own sake, even if it does not bring about any tangible results or personal gain. You get satisfaction from the act of doing, especially if it benefits your community. In this case there may be little or no monetary gain as long as it provides an answer to something that is nagging inside of you. It may well be a desire to test how things could work out if people could be afforded an opportunity to experience something different.

At another level you may be looking around your environment and decide that if you had a lot of money you will put it to good use to benefit your community. You have the desire to give. In this case you start by accumulating large sums of money and when you are ready, you take pleasure in giving it away.

People motivated in this way do not necessarily start off by giving but wait until they have the kind of financial base that will not easily dry out, enabling them to give continuously.

LEADERSHIP: is displayed by people who like to be in charge of situations. They tend to want to have control and an effect over other people. This is being able to affect behavior of others as you are in a position to exert power or have the opportunity to do so.

Leadership is shown by those who work well with others, not just to ensure that they peacefully work together, but being able to positively influence others and get the best out of everyone. Their satisfaction comes from seeing other people achieve their best. This will require having others succeed before you can be personally fulfilled.

Those motivated in this selfless way never seem to run out of people to develop. Seeing others get up and do things for themselves feeds their motivation, and they keep getting more to work with. Overall, they tend to develop leaders instead of followers.

FEELING: This is very strong amongst men and women who are good in sport. Any measure of success, great or small makes one want to get up to experience success again. Winning becomes a drive, and you do not go into any venture for anything else but that. Past successes are not enough for people who are driven by feelings. Every venture is important and special and would get all the necessary attention that will ensure success. They gain satisfaction from both the chase and successful closure. For them, any other rewards are incidental.

These are people who would never settle for handouts. For them, gaining something without working for it is a let down. They are addicted to the feeling of exhilaration that comes with success. The adrenaline rush is sort relentlessly.

FAMILY: The need to adequately provide for ones family makes many to stand up and 'do' even more where they could have easily spent a day daydreaming or doing nothing of importance. For some people it is not enough to just provide the basics, they have to go beyond catering for their needs and provide for their every want. That is the power of love.

The motivation to gain financial independence for one's family could also be associated with past experiences where one may have been forced by circumstances that made them do without what they considered important. Some people who when growing up suffered embarrassment, although may not have been of their doing, such as where their parents were poor, may grow up not wanting to put their families through the same experience. Often they will be comfortable with a clearly mapped out career that will ensure top financial gain. They are not willing to risk careers that will not guarantee the best for the self and family.

The family motivator finds you reflecting on issues that will take into account personal concerns, experiences and expectations. These would be those experiences of the past that you may want to expose your own family to, and those which you will prefer to avoid. You take responsibility when you clearly define what you want for yourself and those you love. You often do not settle for just your success but make sure the whole family succeeds. In this case you will be driven to inspire and guide them forward.

DISAPPOINTMENT: You may have experienced disappointments and embarrassing moments in the past such as a failed business, struggled through school and college because you did not have good financial support, unable to secure a form of gainful employment you had wanted and many more. Any one of these could be reason enough for someone not to want to go through such an experience again. A failed business in the past could be due to having been run badly – poor business management skills. Instead of abandoning your ideas you can harness the energy of your anger (with yourself) or embarrassment and channel it into something useful. You can turn your past disappointments to work for you.

When you are motivated in this way you use past mistakes and failures to build towards success. You learn from your experiences and get to do things differently for a different result.

When your motivators and values are consistent, you will find that it will be easier to accomplish your purpose. If amongst your values you have creativity, knowledge and achievement, you may be driven by the desire to be recognized. Where values and motivators are not consistent there may be a need to revise either to ensure that you move forward smoothly. For instance if you are motivated by adventure it could be impossible to do much to satisfy this if you value stability or conformity.

Whatever motivates you, will influence your decisions and affect how you behave.

What really motivates you?

You may have a combination of all of the above, only a few of them or you may even feel there are others that are not included here that get you going. Consider what is here and reflect on the next activity.

TO DO

Identify your motivators and determine how well you are taking advantage of your inner drive to accomplish your purpose.

- Rank order the motivators above, (i.e. adventure, recognition, benevolence, leadership, feeling, family and disappointment), in order of importance from 1 to 7 (where 1 is the most important to you and 7 is the least important).
- In what ways are your top three motivators influencing your life?
- To what extent does what you do at present (your job, studies, etc.) allow you to satisfy your top three motivators?

- How is your future likely to be affected by your neglecting your bottom two motivators?
- Which of the bottom four motivators would you like to start cultivating and why?
- Are your motivators consistent with your values? Explain.

Will Yourself to Higher Levels of Performance

'I am just feeling lazy these days'. 'I will take a break from that work'. This is normal for many people, but some people never come back from the break. The work remains undone for long periods of time. In the meantime you feel guilty, the work that you did not do weighs heavy on your mind. You are forced to look for excuses to give for that book you promised yourself to write two years ago; the assignment that was due at work last week which you did not do, and your colleagues had to go through a crisis management exercise to cover for you by giving the boss a second rate presentation; that homework you did not do because there was an interesting program on the Television. The list is endless.

If you wait for the spirit to move you, you may be waiting forever. Nothing starts itself – there is always something you have to do to start it off, providing the 'take-off' energy. You have to learn to move your spirit. Will yourself to stand up and do those chores that you most dread. Do not think about it, just do it. Over time you will mechanically do them and even not realize you do not like doing them. Use the same technique to teach yourself to act in ways you do not like but are aware that you need the skills involved to achieve your purpose.

Motivation does not always precede action. You need to act to get to motivate yourself to action. Once you are started you experience satisfaction that if recognized by others, brings a feeling of accomplishment and earns you prestige. The sense of achievement will then motivate you to do more and better.

Knowing your motivators is not enough. It is action that will bring about the real motivation. Action overcomes fear, builds confidence, brings success and all this will increase your motivation. With motivation you can do anything you set your mind to do. It is only you who can do the brand of work that you want. In a world where we crave closeness, where the presence of others in our lives cannot be guaranteed beyond the moment, it is important to ensure you remain close to the one person who really matters and over whom you have complete control - yourself.

Do what you prefer to do most, acquire the habit to work with it by working continuously. Make sure your motivator works for you. Increase your motivators so that you keep doing. Use the technique acquired in practicing your favorite motivator to start yourself with any other motivator.

Develop a strong will to achieve what you want. A developed *will* shows the following qualities:

- **Enthusiasm and dynamic power** – where you channel your energies toward what has to be done, putting all that is necessary in place to produce results. Showing intenseness in doing things.
- **Knowledge and discipline** – being informed about what is to be done, showing mastery of skills and having the discipline to do what is to be done when it is to be done.
- **Concentration** – having the ability to pay attention to detail and being focused; having staying power. Learning from one's effort, paying attention to what one does so that you are aware of the effect of your

action. Not sidetracked by seemingly easier but unwanted and untested ways to do tasks.

- **Decision making** – being able to make good choices that help you achieve goals; staying with your ideas and not easily swayed by lack of support. Acting on own ideas promptly. Showing resoluteness in dealing with obstacles.
- **Perseverance** – accepting things may not work, but willing to stay with what is to be done even in the face of challenges, being persistent. Never losing sight of the bigger picture and willing to change the way you work to achieve it. Showing patience and endurance to stay on.
- **Innovative spirit** – that comes with being courageous and daring. Taking initiative to do what has never been done before without fear of failure. Showing willingness to take risks and being prepared to keep doing until success is reached. Not intimidated by failure.
- **Visionary** – looking forward in planning to have a job done; being drawn to achieving even as you build for future success. Adopting strategies that show that you learned from past lessons and other people.

All the above are useful and admirable traits that can make anyone very successful. Be inspired by your motivators to acquire the competencies that will benefit you. Your growth will never become complete as increase in competencies adds to your motivation and you will keep doing more and expanding your purpose.

All people can benefit from having a bit of all the motivators. For instance, if your motivators fall strongly in the area of adventure, you cannot always have your creativity be controlled by other people. There will come a time when you will be limited by what they think and other important considerations in the establishment. This is when the other level of adventure has to kick in, the level of autonomy. You will at such a time need to make independent decisions that could include venturing out on your own. If this happens, another motivator would have gotten to be more important to you, the motivator of feeling. You can no longer afford to do less inspiring work as you are now addicted to the feeling of success. The more you do, the more you succeed and as you grow, you crave even more success.

==> As you take advantage of your motivator, you may begin to realise that some other bits are missing. You then need to operate at other levels to be able to feel complete.

==> Allow yourself to grow by increasing your motivators. In that way, your purpose, that which you have to do will never be completed. The reasons to go on will increase with time, accomplishments will be many and the end will never come. Yet you will continue to feel accomplished.

==> Success is never complete. When you reach one peak, another appears in the horizon. To keep going higher and higher you have to keep feeding your motivation.

Personal Checklist

1. Do I have my own position to stand on that will enable me to begin my own works that is unique from others?
2. What skills have I developed that will enable me to carry out my own works?
3. What level of education am I at which will enable me to carry out my work competently?
4. What experience do I have in order to carry out my work diligently?
5. Do I possess a job in order for me to follow and service my dreams?
6. What amount of knowledge do I have that will enable me to interact and carry out the works with dignity?
7. Inner self: What integrity do I have that will enable me to consistently carry out my works with discipline?
8. What gives me momentum to carry out the works on my own?

In this section the reader has now become aware of how to start with what they have, it also helps the reader to be prepared for section II. The indicators on the checklist are made available for the reader to check progress on personal development, and the reader can go further and start to list personal checklist.

Section II

The Power Of Habit

Our habits make us. Habits, whether good or bad determine what you become in life. Your level of achievement is a direct result of what you habitually do.

6

Forming Good Habits

abits are a way of getting used to doing things through repeated use until they become reflex actions. Once a habit is formed, it becomes a spontaneous act, reaction to familiar stimuli that makes it possible to respond to things without conscious thought, the action having become second nature. It means that you always do things in the same way all the time. Those who have the habit of perseverance will always see a task through to completion when otherwise they could have been too lazy or seemingly tired to have it done. We first form habits and habits make us.

All great deeds, whose end result can be seen by everyone, are a product of great determination, perseverance and sheer hard work. These are attributes that have become habits to their possessors. All successful people are recognizable by the precision of actions that have become habit for each one of them. They repeatedly do what they believe has to be done, no matter how basic, forming habits that help them produce results.

Let us look at some examples of habits that we can easily miss for what they are. I enjoy reading and tend to read almost all the time. I tend to read different kinds of books. The habit of reading benefits me because I am able to grow as I gain knowledge and reading skills. It provides security as I stay home rather than on the road, and helps me relieve stress. It is this habit that has made it possible to get to write books – I got to a point where I started thinking about what the different authors write about, how they write it and I realized I could also share my story. It has led to the continued desire to acquire new knowledge. Reading is a habit that has enabled me to achieve in my works.

For someone else the habit could be watching Television. When you get home from school or work you sit in front of the TV and may be staying there until way after midnight. You can now reflect on how watching television for six to ten hours a day contributes to your growth. As you watch the different programs you daily conclude that you have to know more and what will happen next. Having formed the habit you never get enough. May be this is the time you could have used to do something else that contributes to the knowledge you need to effectively interact with others.

Other actions such as smoking a cigarette or turning to alcohol for relaxation are more examples of lifestyles habits taken to negative extreme. They can be regarded as addiction. Smoking may help you relax or think more clearly, yet it has negative consequences. It affects both the active smoker and passive smokers causing health problems. The point is, the act related to the habit can have both positive and negative implications. Whatever you have is a result of what you did or what happened in your life. Every result has a cause – it is your habits that you have to guard.

We have to realize that all habits, good and bad, begin with a single repetition. For the most part, neither form of habit is initially enjoyed. However, once you get used to it, it becomes familiar and comfortable. It is the effect of the habit that requires assessing. In order to achieve your best, review your personal habits and give yourself a chance to take control. Strive to improve your habits as necessary so that you come up with those that serve you best. You have the power to break your behavior patterns. You have the power to break bad habits and to create good ones in their place.

Let your habits work for you

Your habits can cripple you where they lead to negative effects. They could make you do less, avoid responsibilities and generally produce far less than you are capable of. On the other hand habits can drive you forward and make you produce well, stretching your capabilities to realize your potential. You need to look into those admirable habits that can drive you to achieving, helping you grow. Put yourself in a position where you are able to keep enriching your life – growing in your chosen career path, raising your family well and getting the best out of yourself to enjoy the life you lead.

Good habits are those that work for you allowing you to grow to occupy your space. These are the success habits that include thinking good thoughts, decision-making, knowledge acquisition and work habits.

A habit is a product of repeated thoughts and acts. A thought precedes all actions. The most tremendous force in the universe is thought – it makes you what you are. Thinking good thoughts make you think of even more good things to do to better your situation. Positive thoughts of love, happiness and the desire to do good will drive you to always look for the good in all people you are with, appreciating them and loving all things. Nurturing good thoughts directs your actions to be positive. Whatever thought you harbor, you act it. In essence, it is what we do, not necessarily what we say, that reveals our thoughts and feelings. Changing your thoughts will in that way lead to coming up with new outcomes. First change your thoughts and you will affect the outcomes of your situation. People can only do what they are able to imagine as possible to achieve. As such, changing their thinking will change their beliefs and determine the actions they will take.

Cultivating good thoughts and creating an internal environment that brings forth the right words will drive you to seek to get the best out of you. Support these with appropriate actions and these good habits will work for you.

Negative thoughts and deeds can be replaced with good ones, thus anyone can order good thoughts, which will lead to good deeds and you will acquire admirable habits. Good habits build you. They create rather than destroy.

By permitting yourself to consistently harbor negative thoughts such as anger, cruelty, hate, you become an angry, cruel person and you will indeed get to hate the object of your thoughts. When in the presence of those you hate, your words will reflect that hatred. You even get to be angry with all people and all things around you.

Dwelling on our negative thoughts often leads to unnecessary anxiety, greed, envy and the tendency to want to own that which you do not deserve. Negative thoughts lead to seemingly baseless anger, fear and being threatened by insignificant things around you. Unforgiving thoughts occupy your mind, keeping your anger alive, and may fuel more negative thoughts. People who forgive those who injured them are destined for great things. By forgiving others they convert their negative energy to constructively build something good. Those who dare forgive an injury show the desire to grow through positivity. They are more likely to concentrate on important issues that will bring out the best in them. Failure to forgive mainly damages you. It causes personal hurt and leads to loss of peace of mind.

You spend precious time and energy plotting and counter plotting; wanting to cause others damage only to come out the loser.

The habit of work

Constant exposure to a thought and related acts will lead to a habit. Over time you act without even realizing that such a thought has been going on in your mind. You become what you think. Our thoughts reflect our beliefs, what we think the world thinks and what we do in reaction to it. Our resulting actions, when repeatedly displayed become a part of us, get to be associated with the individual and as such become your character.

Those who actively do things acquire good working knowledge of their enterprise. They master the art of good thinking. Their desire to know more and grow in knowledge is relentless. They think about what they do, and not just stumble onto the good results they get in their lives. It is those who keep on top of developments in their field that progress furthest.

All things around us started off as 'just ideas'. Thereafter, someone acted upon them. Many people around us have ideas, and they will admit they are great ideas, yet these remain just that with no results to show for them. What they do not have is the habit of work - the ability to patiently work on their ideas until they yield desired results. Where people fail to follow up on their good ideas with work their ideas die off. It is those people who are prepared to do what it takes to make it work that realize their dreams. Being capable of churning out good ideas is not an easy skill to acquire. Nevertheless, once you formed the habit you have to do something about all the good ideas.

Consider what happens when you have the habit of

withdrawing when faced with a difficult task. The habit serves you in that you do not get to do what you are unable to do or what you are afraid of. However, it is a way of acting that in the long term denies you a chance to develop skills. For those who have the habit to persevere, they have the advantage of getting the result they want. Their work gets done. They overcome the fears associated with non-performance, and they keep perfecting their skills as they become better at what they do. With this habit of doing and perseverance, you cannot just give up and do nothing.

Do not be afraid of making mistakes, otherwise that fear might bring about absolute action paralysis. When you stop making decisions in case you fail you finally lose hope of ever doing things right, thus indeed you become a true failure. To get over the fear of failure, you need to make decisions often and confront your failures by acknowledging that they happen and understanding why they do. Act on what you fear and overcome the tendency to be paralyzed by fear.

The habit of working will progressively uncover potential that otherwise was going to remain hidden. Human potential is not realizable overnight. You work through it over a lifetime. Work provides you the opportunity to achieve your purpose in the process fulfilling your potential as you tap on your talents, abilities and capabilities. The experience of success should make you happier and confident, increasing your willingness to work harder, and more often. Work brings about personal progress, and you become productive. Without work we can never discover and make use of our many talents, skills, abilities and capabilities; we cannot grow to own our lives by achieving our excellence.

Be disciplined and stay with the good habits that will work for you. Would-be successful people show mental discipline such that they get committed to all things they want done and will not stop until it is so. They have a compulsion to get results. Because they are action people they are always driven such that work has become second nature to them - pursuits become habits. They grow to become good decision makers as they continue to make good choices for what they want done and how it is to be done. Failure to make decisions when you have to leads to lost opportunity. Others get to do what you could have done and you mainly get to follow them.

Habits are a way of life and you wont get rid of an unwanted habit by willing it away. It takes a new habit to substitute for an old habit. By repeating any act you wish to adopt and replace your old habit you can replace unwanted habits. First you make your habits, and then through your habits you grow into your real self. It is important to accept that for as long as you stay with habits that do not add value to your life and help you develop you fail to take up your rightful place and be your true self. Good habits define what your future will be like. It is by ensuring that you have good habits that are consistent with your desired goal that you will be able to set up an environment that will make it possible to achieve personal excellence.

==> Let good thoughts dominate your mind to positively influence you. Your mouth always makes known what is in your heart and all your thoughts will be known through what you say.

==> The habit of work sets us up to further tap on and make use of our potential.

==> It is through work that new creations can be made that will better human life. The ability to innovate comes to you as you develop know-how through work.

==> Forming a new habit requires that you repeatedly practice what you desire and with time the habit will become second nature to you.

==> Let the good habits influence your life. They will work for you giving you the results you desire. Bad habits only hold you back making you lose on opportunity to achieve your best.

Personal Checklist

1. What habits have I formed that will enable me to successfully carry out my intended projects diligently?
2. Are my habits consistent with what I want to achieve?
3. What negative thoughts do I regularly have that are likely to hold me back?
4. Do my actions support the good thoughts that I have daily to help me achieve my goals?

The checklist has to help you the reader review how your habits affect your life. The next section will take you further to relate to your attitude. Your attitude can make you or it can break you.

Section III

Taking control of your attitude

Attitudes are mirrors of the mind, they reflect our thinking and influence our actions. They determine how we approach our lives, how we behave and relate to challenges. Control your attitude and set the stage for your life actions.

7

It is your attitude that wins the day

The way people perceive any situation they find themselves in dictates how they react to it and what they become by it. Our attitude informs us how to respond to issues - what the issues mean to us and what we can get from them. When your attitude is right you can do anything. On the other hand, your attitude can cripple you if you choose to allow it to restrict you.

Based on the attitudes one holds toward something or an attitude object, you could think and behave positively or negatively about it. It could be an attitude towards another person, specific group, a thing such as an animal, the environment or a particular job, or for an event. What you say and how you act toward an object or situation indicates how you feel about it. It indicates your degree of like or dislike for it. Through what you say about something others are able to anticipate you likely reaction and the actually actions you take, i.e. your behaviour clearly represents your thoughts. We form our attitude as we either translate what we experience or through observing things that happen around us.

Because our attitudes are learnt, we can change them. By allowing yourself to think positively about any situation you can change the outcomes that in some cases could have been destructive. For instance, just by choosing to have more respect for your environment you could find yourself protecting animals and plants, which before you took for granted. Where you would have cut this big tree in your garden you start to hesitate as you consider how the environment will be affected from aesthetic point of view, how animals that depended on the tree for shelter and food will be affected. Your attitude is reflected through your actions or beaviour. The way you behave mirrors your thoughts.

We have a choice every day regarding the attitude we embrace for that day. One person could translate an overcast and cold day as gloomy and depressing. Yet another person could choose to declare the day as just right for doing all the chores that were somehow neglected the past week and attend to what has to be done with enthusiasm.

The effect of our attitudes can be illustrated through the actions of two people who think of a similar business project but come up with totally different results. Following the conception of their business ideas, one is found after a year, to be working hard at the business, the other behaves like the idea never happened. Why do you think this is so? The first person seems to have turned the prevailing circumstances to work for him or her, whilst the second only succeeded in identifying things that would not have made the business work. Yet similar conditions existed for both - market challenges, financial constraints, workers to manage, etc. So why do they respond differently to the same situation?

The answer to this important question may lie with how each of the two people perceives themselves - the individual's views about the self, how they read existing conditions and the importance each accords them. Although their ideas may be similar, the attitudes they each bring to the situation are different. They are differently challenged by the venture before them. It is not individual talent, for if it were, many would have long succeeded in the same business. It is the inner person who has to work the game plan and figure out how to beat the odds. One looks at the odds and decides to face them square on, the other makes them look too important and insurmountable and eventually it leads to defeat.

Table 7.1 below shows some of the differences that may characterize the two people.

Person one	Person two
is on the look out for opportunity	finds reason to explain away the opportunity
shows competence	seems inadequate
seem informed	lacks working knowledge of desired business
accepts and faces responsibilities	rationalises responsibility
faces inadequacies	reviews and dwells on inadequacies
embraces failure	recoils at the idea of failing
seeks solutions	plays up the problems
thrives on challenge	afraid to face challenge
accepts change as inevitable	prefers things to remain the same
does not believe in impossibilities	rehearses impossibilities
finds pleasure in the goal	replaces goal with pleasure
is purposeful	lacks direction
fulfils commitments	rethinks commitments
finalises own decisions	reverses own decisions
prepared to take on leadership	resists leadership

Table 7.1

The one person who believes that anything is possible will approach the situation with the intention to win as such seeks only to do what supports this. Equally correct is that when you believe it is impossible to succeed at something the attitude you bring to the situation will support this and whatever you do, you will sub-consciously working to make this come true.

A positive attitude does not necessarily mean 'fearless'. Overcoming the fear of failing means you will be less overwhelmed by facing unknown situations. Having the knowledge, skills and the right experiences gives one the attitude that anything is possible. Sometimes whatever scares us the most tests our resolve and strength. And if we pass the test, then we end up where we are really supposed to be. The 'I can do anything' attitude, with good habits, always wins.

When your attitude is right your abilities reach maximum effectiveness and good results inevitably follow. The right attitude will always unlocks the mind, and points one in the right direction. With the attitude of 'I'm activated and I can' the person always looks for answers that will enable them. It is by overcoming the defeatist attitude of 'it won't work', 'it is not how its done', 'we have never done that before', etc. that we get to achieve our goals. Even though some things may have never been done before, a positive mental attitude will drive one to seek how they can be done. When the attitude is right, the right answer shall be found. The way you think and feel determines how you approach life.

As you come up with a thought, a complementary action will be created. Action repeated will create a habit. A habit will create an attitude. In the previous section we looked at how our habits give us the power to do anything we put our minds to. The capacity you develop because of your habits gives you a way of judging circumstances, an attitude that shows how you perceive your ability.

As it all starts with a thought, we each choose our attitude for the hour, for the day, for the year or for a lifetime through our thoughts. You may wake up to an all grey, rainy and cold day, but that is no reason to be miserable. When you tell yourself that things could have been worse, and face that day with enthusiasm as though the sun was indeed shining, you will have a bright and exciting day. You get out of each day what you expect from it - after all you do in each day what you expect to achieve in it. You can begin a year dubbing it cursed and destined to be a disaster. Indeed, all things that come your way, you will regard as disasters and some of your actions will unconsciously contribute to this end.

Great opportunities come to us all, but many of us do not know that we have met them. Any great idea one has, has to be supported appropriately for it to come to fruition. The attitude you have about what you can or cannot do reflects what you believe about what you can do. Your attitude shows a lot about the habits you have formed about issues. Indeed people show a specific attitude for an issue, event and any attitude object. At the end of it all, your knowledge and skills reflect what you allow yourself to experience. Form the right habits by using your knowledge, skills and experience properly.

Emotions such as anger, greed and hate also begin as thoughts. If you allow these to stay with you, that is all you shall be, an angry, selfish and bitter person. A positive attitude that regards negative emotions as an opportunity to find an answer that resolves a bad moment will contribute towards personal growth. Resolve your negative emotions and use the energy you have been using to fan them to do something positive.

Just as with positive thinking, you can grow negativity. An angry person seems to be always on the lookout for things to be angry about. Anger becomes a part of you and you turn into a bitter, angry person. The thing to do is to avoid negative thoughts, replace them with positive ones. Think well of others, wish them well and look for the good in them.

Do not let your past experiences limit you. What you may have thought in the past and prevented you from achieving should not be allowed to continue to hold you back. You cannot control what other people choose to think and do. But, you definitely can do something about your attitude. Take charge and control the way you react to what happens to you. Make the best of each day by approaching it with a positive attitude.

Start each day on the offensive. Think well of what you face. Get up and do what you have to do. Do it now. That attitude will make you a winner.

8

Self confidence

Self-confident people have qualities that everyone admires. Self-confidence is extremely important in almost every aspect of our lives, yet so many people struggle to find it. This is a sad situation indeed, given that people who lack self-confidence tends to find it difficult to be succeed in what they do.

A display of confidence makes others believe in you and would be willing to follow your advice. Your confidence shows your attitude. Others get to respond to what you display and treat you as you portray yourself. Confidence comes to you as you set and achieve your goals as such building competency. As your self-esteem drives you to believe that you can cope with what goes on in your life, you get to master skills that makes it possible for you to achieve. Any successes you experience will keep feeding your confidence.

Even with confidence based on your self-perception that tells you you can do anything, it all turns to nothing when you lack competency to achieve your desired goal. Without underlying competency any confidence you may have turn into shallow over-confidence. It is most likely to lead to upset due to the inevitable failure that will follow. It is important that you have skills that make it possible to do what you have to do. Your skills are fundamental in making you good at what you do and being great in what you become. Without skills you cannot achieve competency. The attitude you have about what you can and should do is closely related to your self-believe; what you think you can do, what you want to achieve and what you actually spend time doing. The attitude you display will compliment the habits you formed.

When you believe in your abilities, that is, those competencies that you use to achieve your goals, you become confident that you can do anything. Such confidence comes to you through all the small achievements you have in your 'success-log'. As you set up to be excellent at what you do, your past successes will give you the confidence you need to achieve it. Since you experienced success before you continue to believe that you will do so again now and in the future.

Work on your confidence

Your attitude towards yourself, towards others and what happens around you determines what you become. With the right attitude, you face challenges and failure confidently knowing it will eventually lead to better things. You learn from your failures, not defeated by them. The habits you develop reflect the state of thought regarding what you had to do. An attitude that drives you to successfully complete a task reflects the confidence with which you approach the task.

When you are confident, you will be responsive and better willing to take risks to change your life. You tend to be calm under pressure, as you believe more in what you will be able to do no matter how difficult it may be. Building self-confidence is achievable. You have to focus and be determined to carry things through. Whatever you have to do to build self-confidence will develop the skills that will start you in the direction of your success. Your confidence will come from real, solid achievement.

To build your confidence you have to start with what you have: what you have already achieved; your strengths; your values – what is important to you and where you want to go; and your habits – what you think about, your behaviours. Use you past achievements to motivate you as it shows that you can succeed at what you want to do. Your strengths will show you what skills you have and you can start with these to develop competency. The habits you formed show you what you repeatedly do and how well you do it will show how competent you are.

Protect your confidence level by not giving in to what you are afraid of, or whatever it is that undermines your confidence. For instance, if your confidence stealers are in the area of fear, isolate your fears. If you find it difficult to join in discussions with your peers, ask yourself questions that will help you get to the bottom of your fear. Let us look at the following situation:

"I am afraid that others will know how uninformed I

am, so I do not usually have an opinion to offer".

Then, get informed. Table 8.1 gives example of what you can do when facing a confidence stealer. Go through the same process with all your other confidence stealers to get to the stage where you have a plan of action to follow.

Identify your confidence stealers and look for corresponding confidence boosters to counter the negative effects. Study table 8.2 that gives examples of some confidence stealers and possible corresponding responses. You have some confidence stealers that are specific to you, find possible responses to counter them.

Situation	How do I behave?
• Always seem vague and uncertain on issues that are raised in formal discussions.	• I get frustrated and shy. • I get inarticulate when I do speak. • I tend to agree with whatever others say. • I cannot generate ideas and make decisions.
What do I need to do to behave the way I want? • I will take time to be informed. • I will follow up on situations so that I become aware of issues surrounding them. • I will test my ideas by presenting them to others. • I will be an active part of the solution. Initiate solutions.	**How would I like to behave?** • Give informed opinion, hold objective views. • Present a calm, unflustered attitude. • Make credible decisions. • Speak up and resist just going with the flow.

Table 8.1

Confidence stealers will include anything that holds you back in any way, preventing you from achieving something. For instance, pretending not to have weaknesses, the fear of making mistakes and fear of looking silly, lack of commitment and lack of responsibility. You can get rid of any confidence stealer to regain your confidence by responding in a way that will directly address it and help you succeed again.

Confidence Stealers	Confidence Boosters
Lack of belief in self	Know your worth - your competencies, values and motivators.
Not aware of your own worth	Keep updating your personal portfolio - be aware of and acknowledge personal successes.
Hiding your weaknesses even from yourself	Acknowledge your weaknesses and plan to get rid of them.
Lack of possibility	Be a possibility builder; - generate your own vision.
Lack of commitment	Build persistence and determination. Accept that setbacks are only temporary.
Lack of responsibility	Do not blame others for your actions - accept consequences of your actions.
Fear of making mistakes	From every failure work out what went wrong and learn from your mistakes.

Table 8.2

Believe in Yourself

Those around you treat you the way you allow them to treat you. If you present low self-esteem, that is what everybody will see and will react accordingly. The attitude you hold about what you can or cannot do will guide others to what to expect of you. In presenting yourself, you communicate your feelings of yourself. Thus, if you think you are no good, then that is what they get and how they will thereafter treat you. When you feel confident you will be a picture of confidence and that is what people will think of you. Others react to what you think of yourself.

The level of belief you have in yourself, and your level of self-acceptance determine how you portray yourself to other people. This is your self-esteem, the way you see yourself and it is a way of measuring how worthwhile you judge yourself to be. When you believe you are not good enough to succeed, or you are undeserving of success due to what you perceive as your right, you tend to work such that you fail to take advantage of opportunities coming your way. You think yourself into taking lesser options that you regard as rightly yours. Where you strongly believe in what you can do and that you deserve to succeed, you are able to face the sternest of challenges and you persevere to win. All it takes is for you to believe you can, and indeed, you will.

People with low self-esteem tend to believe that they deserve to belong 'down' there. Often they find all sorts of reasons why changing their situation is not such a good idea. They believe success is for other people. When you lack confidence you feel inadequate in the presence of those you consider better than you. For the most part, you are unlikely to volunteer to do anything that will draw other people's attention to you. You tend to behave like someone who has lost hope. You show very little energy to do anything, tend to be negative about most things and as such believe nothing will ever get better for you. You accept defeat easily. Even where assistance is offered you are likely to show little enthusiasm and commitment to make it work for you. Low self-esteem makes one feel threatened when it looks like someone wants to change his or her situation. This may be so because you are most probably uncomfortable confronting the unknown, as you do not want to face anything knew lest it requires that you do something unusual and you could fail at it. You avoid drawing attention to yourself.

Where you do not feel good about yourself, you tend to:

- feel that the world around you is hostile and unsafe so you are often apprehensive and expecting the worst.
- find it difficult and time consuming to make decisions. You tend not to make an effort to acquire the decision-making skill as you assume that it is for other people that you regard as better than you.
- be unable to put decisions into practice. This is a problem that is related to fear of taking initiative, as you are afraid of making mistakes.
- become suspicious of other people's efforts to help you in any way. This may sometimes be because you think they are aware you are limited in how far you can go in doing things and are helping you so that they do not live with your mistakes.
- worry a lot about what other people think of you as you often assume they can only think the worst.
- find it difficult to reach out to other people, sometimes hoping no one will notice how uninformed you are.

Allowing yourself to be a loser too often gives you a reputation, you are characterised by failure. You then believe you are one of the many whose role in life is to watch others succeed and do great things. This situation can go on forever, unless you make a decision to turn it around. Choose to do something different that will make a difference in your life.

Your level of success matches your attitude towards yourself. You may have in the past made a decision to put together what led to what you are today. If not, it means you have unconsciously decided you deserve to be where you are now. Whatever the case, it reflects your opinion of what your perceived role in life is - either to fill the bottom rung of the success ladder or to clear the top. It reflects your beliefs about success and failure - there are those who are meant to succeed and those who are meant to fail.

If you believe you can, you will be able to do anything you put your mind to doing. That is the power of positive thinking. Belief releases your creative power while disbelief puts the brakes on. Believe, and you will start thinking constructively. Your mind will create a way if you let it.

The Power of Positive Thinking

People with a positive attitude of the mind tend to show characteristics such as:

- optimism
- strong faith
- perseverance
- persistence
- patience
- tolerance
- tact
- generosity
- kindliness
- integrity
- initiative
- purposefulness
- good common sense

Such people are also able to give praise where it is due.

Taking a chance and engaging in activities that you never did before or those that were never tested, is like taking a leap into the dark. You seem to be guided by an invisible force inside you that steadily propels you forward. This is showing an act of faith which when coupled with optimism gives you hope that what you want or believe in will come to pass. When you have faith in what you do, you believe in its ability to deliver what you expect, you behave as if it has already happened long before it manifests. You tend to think about what needs to be done to fulfil your hope. Your actions concentrate on those activities that will ensure that what you believe in will come to pass.

When you truly believe in something, you go after it with a singleness of mind that shows total commitment to your cause. You are not put off by minor delays or failure, nor do you subscribe to the notion that something is 'impossible' to achieve. You stay on the job until it is done. The challenges you meet, all the minor setbacks you face, you take them in stride, as they are necessary checkpoints enabling you to reassess your strategies for increased effectiveness. You continue to push forward, even if you have to retrace your steps and start over and over again. You keep your eyes on the set targets and all your efforts are aimed at getting there. This is a display of persistence and patience without which many people tend to give up on their work, or change their focus to take the easier way out. Believing in yourself gives you the staying power that enables all your energies to be directed towards the achievement of an ideal. This form of commitment gives you a sort of fanatical fixation on set goals.

Where you feel good about yourself, you tend to:
- √ believe more in your competence and are more willing to take risks.
- √ be more energetic and alive, and as such ready to take on most challenges.
- √ seem more open and think yourself as having a lot to offer other people and much more free with your appreciation of others.
- √ have an active imagination and follow through on your thoughts.
- √ be more open to feedback and suggestions from others and more willing to accept criticism.
- √ feel you can face challenges as they arise because you are confident that you will do your best.
- √ believe more in the inevitability of change.

To achieve the positives that go with a desirable image of self, eliminate negative habits, undesirable thoughts and actions. Negative emotional reactions such as anger, hate, selfishness and self-pity lower your self-esteem. They lead to resentment and hatred, feelings that are draining on emotions. Completely eliminate what you despise and replace it with the good you yearn for. Consistently practice what you desire to be and it will come to you.

Build consistency in behaviour

Positive people are prepared to sweat it out no matter how long it takes. They do not need instant results to satisfy themselves. They exercise patience, and believe in success being a process requiring time and a lot of hard work. They remain hopeful that if they keep working towards achieving their goal, the future can only bring great rewards and are willing to wait. They stay with their plans at all times - and are committed to their cause, not just being involved in it. This is a show of discipline without which big rewards that come through hard work can never be achieved.

You draw your self-esteem from your own values, those qualities you use to judge yourself and others by. Where a quality you value is well supported by your actions and is reasonably fulfilled (see list on page 11) your level of confidence will be boosted. However, where you find that you have a low rating for a quality you value, it will have a significant effect. You will be continually nagged by the poor outcomes in an area you would have wanted to excel in. To remedy the situation, you have to find a solution that will bring consistency. The overall effect of this is that you will feel there is harmony between your desires and your ability to achieve. That is, when you believe in your competence, it grows and will continuously be reinforced by the success you enjoy. Your confidence will continue to grow in proportion to your level of success. So success, no matter how small, is important for building confidence, which in turn ensures a growing self-esteem. When your self-esteem is high it often does not seem like a disaster that you fail once in a while.

Being multi-skilled is important in that it gives you choices. It allows you to feel you have alternatives open to you to reach an endpoint in any venture. It continues to add to that positive self-image. Where people have limited choices, they tend to have chronic low self-esteem, often showing itself in the form of inferiority complex.

To grow your confidence, you must first take advantage of your strong points. Succeed, even if it is on small things and allow the small successes to feed your confidence. Get informed about your area of interest, and in the process build a positive mental attitude about yourself as you picture yourself successful in that area. Get help from other people whom you consider successful in your area of interest. Read books and listen to tapes that will do the same for you. Practice what you learn immediately, for action will help you overcome fear of dealing with the unfamiliar.

Win often, even if it is in only small ways, and this will continue to feed your confidence level. In time you grow to trust in your abilities as you can reliably get what you want. Even all others that you work with will continue to prefer to work with you based on the consistency you show.

Reflection

- Is there anything that you now feel you have to change to increase your success?
- Draw a plan to get more information about the area you are concerned about.

Any form of success will continue to feed on itself, for as the saying goes, 'nothing is more successful than success itself'. To help this along:

==>	Keep your mind off negative thoughts and feelings of inferiority.

==>	Keep your thoughts on those things you should want.

==>	The thoughts that you allow to keep running in your mind should be those that will help turn your belief system around.

==>	Believe more in what you can do and less in what you cannot do.

9

You can't win them all

People everywhere face problems in different forms and of magnitude. No one can live a life than moves forward smoothly with out problems to deal with. Problems are a way of nature keeping us alert and aware of our environment. Otherwise without problems we are likely to drift through life blank and mindless with no need to engage, to plan, re-direct our actions and enjoy the euphoria of success.

You are aware that, around you, there are people who are successful and those who are not. There are those who are sickly and those who are healthy, and many more. The difference among the different groups is that those who are doing well have learned to face and overcome a lot of problems. These could have been health challenges where one grows to know how to manage their health; resolving conflicts in the family, workplace, or community; convincing someone to supply you with raw materials for your business; selling your products, and etc. Those who choose to ignore and not resolve problems will get to realise that their situation will at best stay the same, but often it gets worse. Problems never go away when not attended to. It is responding to a problem that gives you the skills you need to handle the same or similar issues in the future.

Taking soft options does not always give greatest rewards, but facing and planning to win in the face of opposition, discouragement due to personal losses and misfortunes will. The actual winning often makes you value the time and energy you invest in finding your way through problems. It makes you acquire personal knowledge, skills and experience which otherwise would never have come to you in any other way. It affects your attitude towards yourself, what you can do, your attitude towards others and life in general.

Giving in to your circumstances and choosing softer options is like what a river does. It chooses the route of least resistance, flowing down slope. A river never flows upwards against the gradient; the challenge is too great for that. If you look at it closely, a river has less character than a mountain. It is only the volume and speed of water that makes it ominous. Why else is it so crooked? The mountain, on the other hand, had to push against tons of earth. It was formed under great pressure and very high temperatures to emerge big and strong, exactly where it chose to emerge. It shows some character.

We all face challenges at one time or the other. The important thing would be what you become because of them rather than what they stop you from doing. If we all succumb to difficulties we face, we will lose control of our lives. We tiptoe around issues hoping they get resolved in some instead to taking charge and make things turnout as we would prefer. Use challenges faced as motivators for increased performance. Accept that there is no success without sweat. You cannot sail smoothly through life without facing storms, each of which will leave you stronger and wiser. To live a life without having to resolve challenges is most likely to mean passively accepting what comes and settling for very little. There would be nothing to cause discomfort that could drive one forward to seek solutions to a problem. You will be indifferent to any ups and downs in your life and would be willing to drift on settling for whatever happens to you. It could lead to one being apprehensive all the time wondering what will happen next.

Develop success habits and be prepared to live up to your own expectations. Do not buckle under at the first sign of opposition. Challenges are there for you to deal with and win. Integrity and the ability to perform in times of problems are clear signs of strength and viability. If you consistently deal with problems you become skilled at it and your attitude towards challenges will be such that you welcome them for what you perceive as their worth.

Reflection
- Do you usually look for an easy way out when faced with challenges or do you meet them head on?

Show Persistence and Determination

Both the flowing river and the mountain succeed because they persist with what they intend to do. However, unlike a river, a mountain shows more determination in that it will emerge at the exact spot it intends to even if it means there is already another mountain there.

Those who do not persist with what they intend to achieve are more likely to give up on their dreams and settle for second best. Situations that might lead to this include being unable to face stern challenges surrounding the original plans and looking for softer options, being impatient and failing to wait for appropriate and expected results. This is when those who are determined to get what they want will seek appropriate alternatives and continue with their original plans.

Determined people are driven to achieve set goals as such tend to be very persistent. Determination drives you on to put your resourcefulness to the test so that you seek new and different ways to solve problems you face. People of determination never give up; they stay with a challenge until they win. Persistence and determination are the two qualities that are consistently found in successful people. It goes beyond talent, genius or even education. These will remain in you or are yours forever, but if you do not stretch yourself to tap into and make use of them they remain there. If you fold in the face of challenge and not find ways to use your special gifts you will never realise your potential. Talent, genius and education are important. But it is having the patience to stay on and make sure they are turned into a useful product that will make you successful. There will always be challenges on the way to achieving success. Expect this and learn to handle challenges for a rewarding life.

Handling problems

Take time to write down your dream - it can be in the area of new employment, career advancement, a new business, and etc.

Give reasons why you desire to fulfil this dream. Make sure you include:
(i)   how you will put it in place.
(ii) possible challenges you may face.
(iii) what you will do to overcome possible obstacles.

The exercise above will prepare you to anticipate possible challenges in line with activities you have to undertake and will help you to be persistent when dealing with problems. Each of the alternatives in front of you will come with challenges.

Always remember that when a challenge does arise, it is not the challenge that may be the real problem but you. How you actually handle any situation you are in will determine successful closure or its persistence. Hasty decisions may lead to covering up real issues and these will later come back to bother you. Allow yourself to be calm before you tackle problems. This could include getting out of the situation for a moment so that its likely overwhelming effect is reduced – take a walk, exercise, or watch a game. Do whatever works for you. Think calmly about the problem and allow others to input into it if necessary. Always consider a problem an opportunity to come up with new answers and acquire knowledge and skills rather than a form of tribulation. It is then that you will get a balance you need to start asking the right questions to guide you to your answer. Gather facts about the problem and come up with a plan of action. Execute you plan with confidence and calm.

Learn from mistakes and grow

People may tell you how something is done, give you necessary instructions to follow, but it rarely makes you produce the quality that is expected. Teachers may relate well to this. For instance, teachers work hard in helping students write quality compositions. In fact learners are expected to start with compositions from a very early age. Yet, even when they sit for examinations ten or twelve years later they do not always do a good job of it. These students would have been instructed on what a good composition entails. So, why do they continue to do badly at it? It has a lot to do with not being given adequate chance to make mistakes and to learn from them. Children are afraid to score low marks. That is what the school system teaches them. The teachers react by showing disappointment and some will scold and ridicule those who dare fail. As such students find ways of pleasing the teacher without making mistakes, in the process, they do not get to experiment on their ideas. They forfeit the opportunity to make mistakes and to learn from them. This is true for all subjects. Children get to do the real learning outside school when they foul up on the job.

No one can successfully get to the top without making mistakes. Expect to make mistakes and be willing to learn from them. Making mistakes is a major part of life. In fact the most successful people make more mistakes than those who do not do well. It is those who are willing to take chances, no matter what the outcome that will grow more in their chosen field of work than those who do not dare. The latter measure their success by the few foul ups they make in a day, or in a week, in the process having maintained their level of performance. This will be true, no matter how low their level of achievement is. Successful people are risk takers. They are not fazed by failure; they use it as a fertilizer to grow their imagination. It is people who make a lot of mistakes who grow to realise their potential. Those who exercise caution will make only a few mistakes or none, and would indeed have reached stagnation. If you are to grow, take risks. Any mistakes you make, let them be a lesson to you.

Since we grow up in a system where making mistakes is regarded as bad, most of us are unable to grow through making mistakes. This calls for changing our views of the importance of taking risks and how one perceives mistakes and failures that will inevitably follow. The mistakes we make should be learning moments, helping us get better at what we have to do, making effective choices and helping reduce mistakes. What matters is not how the mistakes you make affect you in the short term, but how you react to them and what you become by them. To learn from a mistake, work out why it had not been the best decision to start with and on the basis of that make alternative informed decisions.

An attitude that strives to gain experience will help you achieve your personal best. This would be the attitude that realises that challenges are not only inevitable but also a way of bringing sparkle to our lives. The brilliance with which you grow to handle challenges is the experience that gives you your competency.

Those who succeed know how to learn from challenges they face daily:
- ==> They have mastered the art of decision-making and can make informed choices.
- ==> They are informed about what they intend to do.
- ==> They know their strengths and how to take advantage of them.
- ==> They know their limits and which of them to ignore or use this to explore possibilities to develop further.
- ==> They are not discouraged by failure, and they learn from their mistakes.
- ==> They are prepared to start all over again if that is what it will take for them to achieve their purpose.
- ==> Those who never make mistakes are those who exercise caution at all times.
- ==> Learn from the mistakes you make and develop a success system that will serve your needs.

Personal Checklist

1. What are my perceptions of success that allow me to be daring to take on new challenges?
2. What self-image do I hold that keeps making me do things that hold me back?
3. What attitude do I have that supports positive habits that drive me forward?
4. How well do I respond to setbacks to make me take advantage of such moments to start afresh?

It is our attitudes that make us do things the way we do. Our fears, expectations and hopes drive us, and by adopting a positive attitude we can achieve great things. In the next section we will get to look at how giving our very best can greatly benefit us.

Section IV

Always Give Your Best

Giving one's best is about building the self. Give yourself a chance to grow your expertise by doing what you do extremely well. Use your talents well and own your life. The essence of perfection is never reached, but you gain character by trying to reach it. (W. Clement Stone)

10

Going the extra mile

Doing what you have to do on daily basis may seem to be the thing to do because it is expected, it is what you are paid for, or it is what you want to do. However, this may not be enough if you expect to make progress with your job, encourage others to keep working with you, and feed your confidence by pushing yourself to find what you can really achieve. To go the extra mile we dig deep inside ourselves to find ways to do our very best to bring about pleasing outcomes that may have otherwise eluded us. To do this we draw from our strength, often testing our integrity, showing great determination and guts.

Going the extra mile calls for doing more than the familiar and beating personal best. In order to excel, do what you do well, give it all that it deserves and you will be rewarded with the best. However, even if you do nothing and give it 'your everything', failure is what you will show for it. You nevertheless would not want to excel at nothing.

We each of us have our strong points, areas in which we are talented. If we isolate these and create opportunities that will enable us to perform in these we cannot go wrong. For some of us success could mean performing well in the area we feel we are talented in. Relating well to others could be someone's target. Therefore, doing it exceedingly well could be achievement enough for her or him. For somebody else giving their best in all areas of their life could be the aim. Then they have to find a balance that will drive them forward as desired.

In business, it is what you know about it, related skills to deliver on it, and your attitude towards your client that will take you to the top or leave you a failure. To give your best, find out what you need to do in related and key areas so that you meet the varied needs of those you work with to enable you to achieve your goals.

When you are driven to give the best you strive to do so for everything that you do. When one area of your life is lagging behind it reduces your effectiveness. Just as you set goals for the different areas of your life, you have to achieve success in all of them. To get the best out of and for yourself, you have to operate on more than one single, all-encompassing goal as the answer to your life needs. You need many goals that will ensure continued growth, where success for you remains doing better than your last achievement. You develop the drive to reach perfection through setting out to beat personal record achievements. It is for that reason that you must be prepared to put in place, strategies for continued improvement. This is the only way to ensure your continued success. Where there is only one goal, you may achieve it within a year, or two, then you will be at a loss, wondering what else to do. As such your personal best gets to be continuously doing better than your last performance.

Those who do what has already been done, what everybody else does, will only get what others get too. However, anyone who has a burn to blaze a trail never traveled has to do something different, more than usual and better than before. Doing the best at any time may not be enough. It may well be ordinary and whatever you are doing may be looking for something spectacular to impress. The best at any time may not be enough to overcome obstacles. It is going the extra mile that may bring in the additional push to get ahead.

Success is never complete. Circumstances present themselves every time you serve or work with others. There is always more to do, more to gain, more to perfect. The attitude of giving your best raises your alertness to taking advantage of any opportunity that arises, which may allow you to do something out of the ordinary. As you work on one task, you discover more that needs to be done; you find new ways to enhance what you started. Even when you have a working system that suggests that you give good service, you can do that something extra that makes what you do special. Thus you always have more to do rather than find yourself with a completed task and at a loss what to do next.

Giving excellent performance is not about being 101% better at one thing but being 1% better at a hundred things. It allows you to develop a wide range of skills and experiences. You will be able to draw from varied experience to create your special products. When you actively do, you learn. Do not let your learning just lead to knowledge. Let your learning lead to action. The extent of actions you take give you the exposure and experience for what you intend. The measures you set for yourself will give you the feedback you need to show that you are succeeding. Success differs from person to person in different circumstances. Settle only for your own brand of success, and that, always something definitely better than before.

Going the extra mile pays off. It is important to realise that at times it could pay off in the form of personal satisfaction that you made another person happy or that you helped someone complete a task, or simply completing a task in a way that pleases only you. When you stretch yourself to achieve this, you grow in confidence and will in future build on this. In some cases giving your best pays off handsomely. It could come through more people seeking your brand of product or wanting to work with you. The gains you make because of the quality of your service will be higher than if you had stayed with giving ordinary service.

Going the extra mile is not just about deciding to act on the spur of the moment. It is the giving attitude that incites you to action, your way of perceiving situations would be that of making it better for others. Thus, the power of going the extra mile is always something more, always empowering and making things better for all others and the self.

11

Win-win attitude

Learning to put other people first teaches us that our success comes about because there are other people around who contribute to it. We win because there are others involved in what we do, and without them we experience isolation and loneliness that can only be relieved by reaching out to them. The individual's success is best appreciated when others share in it. You win because all others involved win too. The generosity you show when you work with others draw them to you. This is the win-win situation that rewards everyone. Success is based on providing a service, which will be rewarded, and the provider of such service will be the recipient of the reward. Those who you give get satisfaction from receiving and their gratitude, what you are paid now and in the future are your rewards. Win-win is a paradigm. It is a mindset that will see you approach situations with the attitude that there is an abundance of resources and there will be enough for everyone. It is by getting others to win together with you that you really win.

To get what you want in life, help others to get what they want. Give selflessly of yourself. The more people you help, the more you add to your success bag. Put other people's interests, comfort and concerns ahead of yours in the way you think about them, and you will be able to support this with the right actions. Learn to ask the right questions to be able to understand how others think. Then the right answer will present itself.

To get to adopt a win-win attitude you have to cease to be the person who matters most, but become the one who makes others feel important and valued. You have to learn to care when it is called for and be prepared to give than to receive. Your reward will be an even bigger price of success in the future. Our success is a result of how people respond to what we offer them. To show that you care for others goes beyond smiling at them. By selflessly contriving situations to benefit others and you not being the primary benefactor, it shows that the other people involved are important and you care what happens to them. Caring is about feelings and actions that are interpreted as caring by the recipient. When you have done it right you will get the other person to genuinely smile back.

As you go for personal excellence, remember that the greatest victory you have to win is over yourself. There is no win-win if you intend to beat others to win the gold. Compete against yourself, improve the service you provide others, better your previous performance – these will make you give your personal best. In the process help others win too. If they realise that they win when they work with you they will desire to keep working with you, be willing to come back to you for your service, even when they pay for it. They will recognise the advantage to themselves of what they receive from you or what they pay for. On the other hand, you cannot afford to be overly cautious if you are to break world records. Even then, as you take risks to pave new ground, you have to remain considerate of others, as they are the ones to support you to get to where you are driven.

The win-win attitude can be well illustrated in team sports. To get to be the best in team sports, you have to learn to work cooperatively with others. You cannot go it alone. Award winners tend to get their teammates to do their best too. By making the other person shine you make your light more visible. It is when you help others to do well, not to look bad, that your game gets to be good and that is how you will be judged. There is no room for selfishness in teamwork; you have to be supportive at all times. We are interested in others when they are interested in us. We choose to work with those who are welcoming. By supporting others they will make your star shine even brighter.

Make them feel good

Through your actions, others get to realise you care, and that makes them feel special. On providing a service, you aim at serving other people's needs. Your customers will be delighted if you provide a little more than expected; a service excellence that will make them seek more of the same from you in the future. For instance, service could be providing entertainment, selling goods or training. Whatever it is, do it well and delight your customer.

Have something positive to say to your clients as you serve them and when you part. Be genuine with your client at all times. Give those you work with time and quality attention, listening and responding to what they say. You may know a lot about the business you are in, but it is not your taste and interest that people will necessarily want to receive or pay for. Their desires have to be catered for and as you work on ways to meet these, you are likely to help your business grow as new things and new ways of doing things are brought in. A win-win attitude calls for looking for ways to cater for diverse needs, making it possible to innovate.

Avoid standard phrases or routine activity when you deal with your clients. Work out what each needs and respond to it. Some clients need to be chatted to whilst others may consider it a waste of time; some need to be left alone and they will talk to you when they are ready whilst others need to be approached; some need to be directed to get to a decision whilst others already know what they want and would prefer you to do what they suggest. Make them all aware that you are ready and willing to help if and when they need you. By allowing what each desires to direct your service you please the most important person in your business – your customer. By adopting the attitude that gives, it elevates you in the eyes of all others; it helps you 'up' your game to satisfy needs of those you work with. You gain the all-important experience of how to handle the different types of people you encounter.

The people you serve judge you on what they see, your behaviour, your attitude as they perceive it and what they get out of it, and never on your intentions. Provide good service first, fulfil your promise beyond expectation and your reputation will be made. Let your word be your honour. That is how in business you will be able to keep your customers. The most effective form of advertising is the quality of service you give.

Always communicate interest, concern, enthusiasm and the willingness to go the extra mile. Make the people you serve feel that they matter to you and you are glad they are with you right at that moment. Make them realise that they have made the right choice to be with you. You can choose to only cause mild ripples in the lives of people by providing service in an insignificant way; or you can create waves and touch their lives in a memorable ways by paying a little more attention to the quality of the service you provide.

Those who provide first class service get to enjoy satisfaction that comes with knowing they have given their best and made someone happy. Those who are served well can be relied upon to come back for more of your brand of service. They are often willing to encourage others to get to experience the same. There could be no better advertisement than real life testimonies.

Make them feel good, loved and cared for. It will be enough for most to do everything in their power to return the favour even if it means extending the same to someone else. By building excellent relationships you extend yourself, surrounding yourself with others who can in turn share whatever they have for the benefit of all.

Shoddy work is a sign of disrespect to both the self and those you serve. In this case you have failed to teach yourself what really counts as 'excellent' and what would be considered 'substandard'. Is there a good way of doing things and yet a better way of presenting the same? Where you do not pay attention what these things mean, you do yourself a disservice. When you deliver poor service it reflects your attitude toward the work itself, the people you serve, and it could simply be a reflection of your state of mind, a troubled mind at that. It may be unresolved personal problems or issues that you have to deal with in order to lighten up. Get rid of the excess baggage in your mind that clutters it and prevents you from setting your priorities straight.

An indifferent approach to your work or approaching yourself where you portray the attitude of 'victim' may be some of the reasons you give poor service. You give the message that 'you are not where you are by choice, you are fulfilling somebody else's desires'. A winning attitude gives a completely different message. You get over the self-pity and cease to consider yourself a victim but a winner who can make the world a better place where there is enough to share. Should you choose to give the best, you get to focus on other people's needs and take a break from the concerns and worries about your life. Although it may be temporary, with time, the lightheartedness gets to replace the gloom.

- √ Start by choosing a better attitude, an attitude that is intending to deliver good service.
- √ Adopt a positive attitude that will enable you to approach your work with enthusiasm and desire to serve well.
- √ Love what you do and do it efficiently and effectively.
- √ Overcome the reluctance to learn what you have to do and know where you want to go.

You will do well if you start by choosing to love your work. We sometimes find ourselves doing work that if there was a choice we would stay as far away from as possible. Although we may not always be able to choose our work, or what we do when we are at work, we sure can choose how we approach the work. This could come in the form of avoiding unnecessary interruptions and delays. You have to make sure that you decide on what you will do in each day before the day starts. Stick to the days plan and let any newly emerging needs of the day be attended to together with or after your important tasks are done. You attitude will communicate your desire to serve and rid yourself of giving unnecessary excuses. Choose a positive attitude that will always help you get through each day. And you will always get the best out of each day amongst which will be a lot of smiles and good will.

Avoid pushing the nasty chores, those activities you do not like to late in the day. That would be a sure way of avoiding them. 'Swallow your frog' first thing in the morning then you have the rest of the day to attend to more pleasant activities. Make up your mind about what you are going to do and do it. This is a way of deciding to be decisive. Think through your idea, try it out and see what comes of it. Based on the result, adjust or modify your actions until you get what you want. This is possible when you do not suffer 'perfection paralysis'. That is when you realize that you cannot always be correct. Some of the things you do will go wrong and in fact only a few will ever be right first time around. Do not stumble on what you get on each day. Make a deliberate plan and be clear what you would like to see happen to and for you.

When you choose your attitude you demonstrate a level of personal accountability. You show that you are proactive and in the process you release the hidden energy that you will need to positively embrace those you serve at all times; you also ensure that all your best qualities are fully utilised.

A win-win attitude can really make everyone a winner. You have to understand that there is no room for compromise that may turn one of the parties into a victim – the one to lose as a way of making someone happy. There is always enough for everyone. For as long as the intention is not to suggest that the same things can satisfy all people, we can definitely find ways to meet everyone's needs. In making everyone win you would have had to find and utilised different ways to do things. It all requires that you find novel ways of doing things as such extending you to put together hitherto untested ways of doing things. It tests your skills and gives you new competencies that will continue to serve you in the future.

As you serve others well, you get to:
> ==> learn to do a good job.
> ==> experience the joy of seeing others accept and enjoy what you offer.
> ==> grow as a person as you perfect skills.
> ==> improve your creativity and innovate as you get to put more new ways of doing things in place.
> ==> just be happy to be alive and useful to others.

If you do it right you get closer to understanding the joy of giving and being appreciated.

12

Be a team player

Although the idea of a team is often associated with sports or the work place, a good team player starts at family level. We each have a role to play as a daughter, a son, one of the siblings, a spouse and in an extended family circle. We tend to place different emphasis on what each team player has to do in different team settings because we each have to do it well wherever we are. And when we do the team will work smoothly and grow to achieve its goal.

A good team player keeps up with the team's set objectives and pace. To be able to do that you have to be prepared to give up anything that holds you back. To effectively play your role you have to acquire the right skills and grow as needed; be aware of necessary developments so that you may change and do things differently when called for to get different results. The desire to hold on to old practices can stop you from joining in as others work towards the set targets. This more so if you are set on doing the routine, staying with the familiar even when it is not giving the result you want and when you do not have your eye on the set goals.

Each team player has to know his or her role and how he or she fits in with the others. A winning team cannot afford to duplicate roles and leave other roles unattended. Knowing where you fit in will allow you to suitably gauge how suited you are to be one of the team and how to help the team to apply itself. Indeed, even at family level we do not expect a parent to abdicate roles and choose to behave like one of the children.

How to be an effective team player

We each have a role to play in a team and whatever your position you have to assume responsibility and play your part well. You have the responsibility to inspire and motivate your teammates not necessarily as a team leader but as a member of the team. The success of a team depends a lot on the effort of all its members. It is important that you become an effective team player doing your fair share of pulling others along so that everyone gives peak performance. Following are qualities of an effective team player.

1. **Demonstrates reliability**: can be counted upon to deliver good performance all the time – he or she follows through on assignments, does fair share of work, works hard and meets commitments.

    — Give your best at all times.

2. **Communicate effectively and constructively**: shares ideas with others easily both formally and informally. He or she expresses thoughts and ideas clearly, directly, honestly and with respect for others and for the work of the team. He or she is a disciplined listener who allows for meaningful dialogue. He or she can absorb, understand and consider ideas and points of view from

other people without undue debating. He or she can receive criticism without reacting defensively.

— Be open and share information freely with others. Ensure that others get necessary information in good time for them to meet their targets as expected.
— Assist others as and when it is needed.
— Build strong and productive relationships by being supportive of others. Be the anchor that ensures others do well in given assignments, and ensure that you are respectful of the efforts of others.

3. **Exhibits flexibility**: a good team player is adaptable and does not hold rigidly to a point of view that needs changing or improving, especially when new ways of moving forward are needed. Is open to what others have to offer even when he or she shows firmness and consistency of thought.

— Respect ideas forwarded by others without favour.
— Be open to other people's suggestion and feedback. Adapt and adopt suggestions and feedback you receive from others to improve your performance and influence that of others.

4. **Cooperates and shares openly**: is able to figure out how to work well with others to accomplish set goals. Is prepared to assist those who need help and offers to help openly. Willingly shares information, knowledge and experience with colleagues. Is always consistently courteous and considerate.

— If you are good at something, share it with others by coaching and training them as needed. This will greatly enhance your knowledge.

— Identify a junior member who can benefit from your expertise and help them learn what is required. Your protégée will be open to work with you and assist you in the future when you might desperately need it.
— Collaborate with colleagues and communicate successfully. Know when and how to give room for others to give their best performance.
— Be prepared to take instruction graciously. Realise that others may know more than you do and have to be granted due respect.

5. **Participates actively**: A good team player prepares well for team events and activities such as meetings where he or she is able to listen actively and participate in discussions. He or she always does fair share of assignments and would volunteer for assignments.

— Take initiative to improve a situation and set things right instead of waiting for others to do it. Taking initiative will provide opportunity to innovate.
— Do well all the work that you are assigned and be available to volunteer for new assignments. By giving quality work you raise the bar for all others and would drive the team higher.
— Keep your eye on and deliver on the bigger picture.

6. **Shows commitment to the team**: A good team player cares about own work, that of the team and is interested in individual team members. Good team players give their best and want other team members to do the same. They readily subscribe to win-win outcomes because they seek mutually beneficial solutions; they look for the good in others rather than their faults; they are intent on finding solutions to problems and would

collaborate with others to find solutions rather than
dwell on blaming others.

— Be generous with your praise giving credit where it
   is due. Never take credit for any work that you did
   not do.
— Pool resources so that you take advantage of all
   available expertise to do a job well.
— Be generous with others and make their work easier
   where needed.
— Make use of your best skills to the maximum.

Experience growth at all times. Once you feel you have
arrived and there is no growth, worry that something is
wrong. A good player always look out for ways to develop
further and keep getting more out of self and others.

Most people need to belong, where they feel wanted
and needed. They want to be valued as members of a team
and will always respect those who make them achieve this.
Encourage others to give their best, make them recognise
their potential and help them deliver on their potential. The
basis of a powerful, supportive and lasting relationship,
whether it is in business, at personal or family level, is to
seek to support and help the other person fulfil his or her
most important values as much as you can. The skill to do
this for others will set you apart from the ordinary team
members. Helping others to be bigger, can only add to what
you already are.

Moving beyond doing the expected and beating set goals
without upsetting others is a mark of personal excellence.
It allows you to search farther and find creative ways of
solving problems. Your self-confidence increases through
any success you achieve no matter how small. Improved
self-image will enable you to push your creativity and keep
innovating as needed. You draw strength from within you,

which enables you to exercise tact even when pointing out the shortcomings of others.

When you believe in your own capabilities you get to display patience, tact and tolerance, you will have a high and positive opinion of your own worth, which can never be dented by even the most scathing of comments from others. You believe in and get to know what is right, and can always do the right thing even as you try to do things right.

A willingness to provide help where it is needed comes from a generous heart that can share with, support and build others. Extending a helping hand denotes a mind that believes in the power to generate more as you give. Such people understand the power of praise. They praise lavishly, using it to build other people's confidence.

Working well with others involves being honest and showing that you are morally upright. Where you break promises as a way of getting out of tight spots means that when you are found out you cannot be trusted. With the right attitude, you plan, are able to keep promises and make fair decisions. You earn trust of the people you work with and are respected by them because you show integrity.

When business is failing, managers sometimes look up to consultants to suggest solutions. Often, consultants recommend what is to be done but rarely do they realise that theories may be known but to translate them into winners requires a different kind of person, one who inspires and enthuses those in the team to give their all. This may be you. Play your part well. Be open to try out new ideas.

How well are you doing as a team player?

It is important that team members focus on all the important areas to get to move forward as a coherent unit. You can use the statements below to find out how well you are focused on what matters in your team.

Indicate whether each of the statements is TRUE or FALSE for you:

√ Able to assist others where needed   T/F
√ Am keeping pace with other team members   T/F
√ Work well with other team members   T/F
√ My efforts are well focused on the bigger
  picture   T/F
√ Am growing in my area of responsibility   T/F
√ Am able to consistently deliver to expectation
  in my area of responsibility   T/F
√ Able to identify personal weaknesses   T/F
√ Able to work on personal weaknesses   T/F

All of the above statements have to be true for you to be truly working well with others. Where any of them is false or you have doubts about the extent of your true contribution for any one of them, you have to make a deliberate effort to change the situation. This you can do by finding out more about your area of weakness from any source and working on rectifying the problem. Come up with a plan of action so that you get to do what you may have never done before. Set your mind to enjoy the change. Other ways include working closely with someone who is well informed in your area of interest, a mentor.

Poor team players show some or all of the following traits:

- Do not see the big picture and tends to engage in routine work without showing any intention to make it contribute to set goals; may also reluctantly do work, ignoring timelines because they fail to read its importance.
- The individual fails to grow in own area of responsibility, as such holds others back who may be moving ahead.

Closely related to this is failing to recognise and work on personal weaknesses. Being unable to analyse own situation objectively to get to clearly measure the effect of contributions one is making.

- Being unable to keep pace with other team members and often characterised by late deliveries. This holds the whole team back especially if your contribution is to be built into the final package.
- Refusing to work with the rest of the team which could be because you do not consider them good enough and only your work should be moved forward. Where you have a different agenda to everybody else you are likely to stand out as a poor player.

  You may also not work well with others where you are afraid that you are not good enough to contribute as good a quality as the rest of the team; you do something different so that you are constantly judged differently from others and are not easily found out.
- Being unable to fulfil expectations for own area which could be a sign of lack of competency that could be solved through acquiring the relevant skills.

All team members have to play their part; otherwise they become a burden to others, which is a situation that often leads to resentment as the strong members of the team become tired of carrying the weak members. A weak team member who does not pull his or her weight could easily weaken a team to half its strength or less. This situation becomes even more obvious where teams are small. In such cases, there are few people in the team available to carry the weak person and they are likely to feel the weight much more quickly. It is for that reason that a team is often as strong as its weakest member.

Do not allow yourself to be carried by others indefinitely. Close existing gaps by:

(i)   seeking the necessary information so that you get informed;

(ii)   creating opportunities to acquire the necessary skills and build competencies.

Do what has to be done as that is the way to gain experience. Conversely, find ways to assist your weaker team members to come up to expected levels of performance. Just as others cannot carry you forever, you cannot carry others indefinitely when you are the stronger team member.

Recognise your talent and be aware what your strengths are. You may have the desire to do great things but find that you lack the staying power required to finish them off. This is when you give your best where you can and not stand in the way of those who are better able to complete what was started. Good collaboration skills ensure all people perform in their area of strength for the good of everyone.

Recognise and encourage diversity

In order to achieve set goals efficiently you need to work well with other people. These will be people with different interests, abilities and motivations. To successfully work with all of them, you have to help them to give their very best at all times. You do it right by showing empathy and tolerance of the shortcomings of others and the willingness to take time to help build other people. Tolerating and helping others will also help you grow. By working well with others you test your existing knowledge and learn from your experience. Through experience you keep coming up with new strategies of doing things increasing your competency.

There is a tendency to want to uphold prevailing culture and to expect those around you to do things as you might have done. This has its limitations. It closes off opportunity to innovate. Growth lies with cultivating and not just tolerating differences. Good ideas come from existing 'difference'. All innovations came to being because creative ideas were allowed to flourish and something different was allowed to establish. Therefore, it is in differentiation, not in uniformity, that we can progress. The coming together of different talents has the potential to produce something unique.

Recognise in those around you, their strengths, the way they interpret issues, their fears and for each, give room for them to give their best. Be prepared to find reserve energy to pull up the weaker members, assisting them to come up so that they also get to deliver on what is expected of them. As you inspire others to give their personal best, together you get to learn new and better ways of delivering towards set goals. The satisfaction of helping another person could be reward enough for you. It definitely helps you perfect your 'people skill'. Built into this is improving on your higher skills at the levels of collaboration and communication. A good team player knows how to pull and push others to higher levels in the face of the sternest challenge. He or she Listens and hears what others have to say; gives others a chance to voice their fears, which although may seem small and unimportant to some, they are real to them. The best form of support you can give is to enable others to self-help rather than you giving them what they need only for them to come back for more. Reducing others to being charity cases will over time change their gratitude to resentment.

A good team has to display a number of good qualities necessary if it is to be counted amongst the teams that matter. The qualities include character, competence, commitment, consistency, cohesion and unrelenting focus.

Character - Is shown by the unique way in which members behave as they pull together to achieve a common goal. They show an awareness that the way each person behaves affects others around them.

Competence - Having the right skills that are needed to have the job done and going further to create a competitive force. It includes the development of natural talent of all members and more, where each surpasses whatever they initially brought to the team.

Commitment - Displaying the desire to get things done well where all members pull together, assist one another to ensure they move forward as a unit. The team considers itself successful if all members succeed, not just plod on. They desire and do all things possible to succeed.

Consistency – Delivering the very best at all times. This makes for a reliable record, and those working with you get to know what to expect from you and trust you will deliver to standard. The team has integrity.

Cohesion – A product of everyone taking pride in the team's ability to deliver at a high level and will all do whatever it takes to maintain this. The team builds an inner force that seems to push all members to do whatever it takes to pull through, no matter how formidable the opposition. They have that unique pulling force that remains illusive to outsiders.

Focus – Working towards the set targets without shifting the goal post.

A single person, no matter how brilliant, will find it difficult to match the collaborative talents of an effective team. The team's energies have to remain concentrated on achieving the set goal; only the route to getting there may change in the effort to accommodate others. Create conditions where others are willing, able and accountable to perform to their potential. This is important because a team reaches its maximum best when all its members perform at their personal best.

13

Communicate well

Effective communication is key to success in life, work and personal relationships. Communication is successful only when the source or sender and the receiver understand the same message. Communication remains ineffective when the intended message is misunderstood, frustrates the receiver, turns into error or even a disaster. This can happen when the message is delivered poorly and is misinterpreted. To have an impact through communication we have to develop the skills needed to communicate effectively.

We communicate to people by way of what we do or fail to do, the things we actually say or fail to say. It matters therefore that you communicate clear intended messages and interpret messages from others correctly. With this there will be less chance of being misunderstood. The way you say what you want to say, and do what you want to do sends a picture to the other person that they can rely on and trust you to complete the task and provide a service as promised.

Communication has the power to destroy, or build relationships. It allows us to connect with others, so helps us to establish and modify relationships, build rapport, making it essential that we communicate well at all times.

The way you feel – your confidence in your ability to communicate well, will affect how you actually present what you intend. The attitude you bring to communication will influence the way you approach and interact with others. This in turn will affect the outcome. An optimistic, honest and sincere, and respectful outlook will give an attitude that is sensitive to other people's feelings. When it shows that you believe in their competence others will approach what you present with an open mind.

Acquire advance communication skills. Start with simple interactions at social level to profession communication at work. Focus on the skill you want to refine and use it repeatedly to give it time to take hold.

Each time you use a communication effectively you open yourself to more opportunities and future partnerships. This will increase your confidence and will give you more courage to say what you think. When you know that you can make worthwhile contributions to events it will be easier for you to look into you strong points when sharing your thoughts and go further to identify your specific weaknesses in the way you communicate. Once identified you may be able to work on your weaknesses to get rid of or improve on them. Continue to share your opinions and feelings to improve your skills. Even as you expose your thoughts listen more to receive the benefit of other people's knowledge.

Steps in communicating effectively

On communicating with people, it is important to realise they do not receive information neutrally, nor do people receive information in the same way. The new information has to fit in with the existing beliefs and expectations. People have to be comfortable with the new information, interpret it as sensible, useful and needed. The person communicating also has to be judged as the right person to share the information, showing the right amount of emotional involvement.

Following are steps in effective communication:

1. Know what you want to say and why

Understand the purpose of your message, and know whom you are communicating with and the reason for it. Be clear in your mind what you want to achieve. Know what makes your audience tick, and consider possible barriers that may be due to situational circumstances such as economic, gender and age differences, and cultural differences.

2. Decide how you will say what you want to say

Knowing what you want to say will not be effective unless you say it right to get you what you expect. Assume a calm attitude that allows you to make eye contact and give it an appropriate emotional pitch. You will inspire trust and confidence making the other person more receptive. A more open posture, keeping your arms at your side show others that you are approachable and also open to hear what they have to say. Folded arms, hunched shoulders and wandering eye generally suggest disinterest or unwillingness to communicate. The tone of the presented information should be neutral and non-adversarial allowing the receiver to draw own conclusion. When you are nonjudgmental it helps the receiver to relax and open up for neutral dialogue.

3. Listen well

When you talk to people you expect that they get absorbed in what you say and you would probably be flustered by their wondering attention. Having made your point, it is only natural that you will expect others to react to what you said by processing the information, then showing that they agree or disagree, and making their response known. So you have to listen attentively in turn. Allow those you communicate with to have their say without interruption, listen to everything that is said and not select what you want to hear. To react to responses and what others say to you ensure that what you said was clearly and correctly understood. Ask open questions and encourage discussion. Clarify any areas you have to.

Being fully aware of the response by everyone is critical in ensuring that the communication is effective. It is important that you also listen to what is not being said. It will allow you to respond appropriately when you correct misunderstandings that may stem from unexpressed views. You will be able to bring in new information that will help clarify your point, ask relevant questions to enable you to hear what others know or what confuses them. In the process you learn what others think, how they think and how information you give can provoke other people's minds. So be fully present to make good communication possible. Listen attentively so that you get to hear what is in the silence too.

4. Ensure that they are all with you

Communication is effective if the people involved are authentic, and not pretend to be who they are not or to understand what they do not. After receiving feedback to your message assess it and see if it fits in with your original intent. If you have been understood, questions would have been answered, concerns alleviated and you share a point of view.

You communicate well when:
  — Know what you want to say. If when you talk to others you sound uncertain, even though you had something to offer, they are likely to 'switch off'

wondering why you bothered to talk in the first place.

— Keep it simple. Putting in unnecessary detail may distract or confuse your audience.

— Be accurate. The wrong message may be worse than none at all.

— Use appropriate language. Different groups of people will understand you best if you tailor what you communicate specifically to what they are likely to relate to.

— Decide the best format to communicate what you have.

— Speak or write it out clearly. Use of catchy, relevant phrases and anecdotes enables people to follow what you are illustrating.

— Say it in an appropriate manner - outright and assertively, or sensitively in a roundabout way. Decide when and where it is appropriate to say it. Understanding your audience will help make the right decision.

— Maintain eye contact and avoid staring at the other person or keeping your eye too long on one person in a group.

— Adopt a consistent manner of saying and meaning what you say and be seen to be genuine.

— Respond appropriately to reactions of others. Clarify any point that you may think is confusing as soon as you recognise the need to.

— Adopt an attitude that is not patronising. Carry others with you at all times.

Behave as someone who has something special and important to offer. Deliver it with enthusiasm. Enthusiasm is contagious; the other person will have no choice but to join in.

Are you receiving message appropriately?

- Avoid letting your past experience to interpret messages for you. Start on a clean slate as you deal with other people.

- Get rid of prejudices and unsupported assumptions. Your opinion of the other person may be based on the way they are dressed, the people you sometimes see them with, or even an unfortunate instance in the past that may not necessarily be a true reflection of who they are. If you judge them on the basis of your preconceived opinion, you are likely to always be thinking 'I know what you want to say', or 'I know what you are going to say,' and as such you only hear what you expected. Even innocent comments get to be given unintended meanings and are built into big challenges for you.

- Actively listen to what the other person says to you; show you are listening by repeating or re-phrasing what has been said.

- Ask questions to check out what is being said. This helps clarify issues as they are related to you, besides making the other person feel confident that you are interested in what they have to say. Avoid talking for too long. It takes a big person to monopolise listening and a lesser person will monopolise the talking.

- Listen for feelings behind the words. Sometimes words alone are not adequate to express what we feel. The real message may be in the way we say it.

- Read body language appropriately. For instance, a person talking to you communicating anxiety and fear would be in need of reassurance from you before they get to express their true feelings.

- Avoid being judgmental in reaction to what is being said; this is likely to provoke a reaction you might later regret. As the saying goes, 'Least said soonest mended'.

Communication is key in all our relationships. It starts from a very early age for everyone, and no matter how young one is they communicate to others and expect a response that shows that they have been heard and are appreciated. Poor communication can ruin what could have been a good parent-child relationship, student and teacher relationship, and promising friendships, an effect team, etc. Every situation needs to be understood and appreciated on its own merit as such no one is ever above paying attention to what will make communication effective. There is always something you can do to make a difference and whatever it is, do it well. Communication is an important skill that no one can acquire by just thinking or reading about. Deliberately set out to be a good communicator. Pay attention to what happens during any communication encounter and strive to always do it well for even better results.

> ==> As you receive a message, make the other person feel that at that point in time, they are what matters most to you. Make them feel special.
> ==> When giving or receiving a message, the words, the tone of voice and the body language must all combine to give the same message or show appropriate concern. If any one of them is seen to be out of step the message or your reaction is likely to be interpreted as insincere or be treated as suspect.

14

Own your life

We all want the good in life. All people enjoy doing well at what they set out to do. They appreciate what makes them happy and what brings them closer and closer to achieving their goals. No one likes living under perpetual uncertainty. It is for that reason that we tend to strive for a form of success. Some people seek it through approval of those they look up to, while others determine what matters most to them and goes out to get it.

You can never do well at anything until you actually work at it. Doing your personal best at any time is not something that happens by chance. It is often a result of applying your knowledge and skills in special ways to come up with something unique. The success of the moment is what teaches you how it feels and tastes and you take to it. The natural response is to look for opportunities that will allow you to repeat experience.

Although we are often unsure and not good at doing something new in the beginning, repeated exposure gives us confidence as we hone skills. With time one becomes excellent at what they do. Clearly it takes a lot more than doing to persevere with something given that we do not all succeed at the same things even when opportunities seem to be the same. We each bring to any activity our experiences and respond differently to the same stimulation.

On achieving personal excellence, the way you perceive things and how you present yourself would be consistent where the inner and outer self are concomitant. To reach such a level, you will have to be in full control of your life where you have ensured that you call the shots as you make use of relevant knowledge and skills that allow you to do what you really love doing. It is never enough that you know what to do and have skills to support that knowledge. The very foundation that you base what you do on matters a lot as it enables you to make choices that are credible and support your inner convictions that what you do matters and is worth pursuing.

Take control and own your life

Those who allow life to happen to them miss out on the benefits they could have gotten from actively participating, facing the real choices that lead to successful closure of events. Although they may be counted among those who were there when things happened, they are unable to earn the all important skills and the working knowledge that could have made them different from those who never got the chance. Know what you want to do with your life, pursue it with a passion and ensure you get the result you want.

The price of ignorance can be really high. When you are lacking in knowledge and skills you are most likely to drift with popular opinion of the moment or just wait for others to make decisions for you. You procrastinate, wasting time because you are uncertain what you have to do. Even when you know what the right choices could be, you would most probably make compromises because left to yourself you would not know what to do to get what you want due to lack of experience.

Personal experience cannot be traded for the softer options in life. Experience allows you to be creative in the face of challenges so that you innovate to come up with answers for your life. Without experience, there will be nothing for you to improve to take your life to another level. Challenges and problems faced and sorted out are the bases for all successes enjoyed by the greatest achievers of all time. To be regarded as successful even by yourself as well as by others, set out to take control of your life and own your knowledge and skills. Get to apply what you have to gain experience. You do not own a skill or knowledge until you are able to make use of it in novel situations. Be good at what you do through practice and be on the look out to get even more at every opportunity.

- Visualise what you want, set out to make it possible by knowing what to do about it.
- Do what you want to do well. It will help you keep adding to you experience.

It is only those who have been through the storm that can realistically relate the experience.

Let your emotions be a good teacher

Some find it fitting and justified to lose one's temper. Often the response is 'that is the way I am'. To say that you cannot stand nonsense from anyone is to imply other people do. Yet no one wants the irritation, lack of consideration, the abuse and any form of ill treatment. Besides you may be assuming that what you usually do to others is right and appropriate and are not aware that it is equally offensive to them. They deal with your annoying tendency in different ways. Remember we all experience different emotions at different times and respond differently to similar provocations. We however should not let our emotions control us and even destroy us.

Mastering your emotions is a mark of personal excellence. Negative emotions have to be managed in ways that will lead to you growing by both getting rid of the annoying behaviour and using the signal of the emotion as an indication that you have to deliberately engage in doing something positive to neutralise it. Emotions do not spontaneously flare out. After receiving the stimulus that provokes the anger you have time to decide what to do next. You have to allow yourself to recognise how it feels when an emotion sets on. Deliberately adopt a form of intervention that will enable you to take control. For instance you may choose to slowly count to three before responding to what you consider provoking your anger or making you anxious.

Emotions are closely associated with our feelings, thoughts and behaviours. An emotion can be triggered in response to the need to protect you. We can use the classic example of fight and flight response to fear. When you are afraid, you are capable of fighting in ways you never thought possible and that because you would be aware that doing anything less will harm you or your loved ones. Even if you literally run away from the source of fear you will live to see another day. As such emotions are neither good nor bad; they are neither positive nor negative. They are there to alert us that something is about to or something is happening and you have to pay attention.

You may have realised that a response to any emotion uses energy. A negative emotion can benefit you only if you harness that negative energy and let it work for you. Instead of fanning your anger, feelings of jealousy and hate and selfishness you can instead spend energy looking for ways of doing good that can benefit yourself and others including the object of your negative emotion. Pay attention to how you feel when you have done something good. You may feel light and the act brings satisfaction. Therefore by doing good often you will transform your life since the action you take benefits you. Besides feeling good, you contribute positively to others and you gain skills as you carry out tasks. You win, and others win too since you teach yourself new skills and serve others too.

When you listen carefully to what your emotions tell you, you will be able to find a connection between your values and emotions. You will definitely experience disappointment when any of your values is violated. You may even have experienced reluctance to go against your own convictions before it happened. By paying attention to the warning signal you prevent the damage that may be caused by the unwanted emotion. Be grateful that you experience emotions. They are your wake up call to be alert that you have to make a choice.

Our emotions can teach us a lot about us and we can learn great lessons from them that will lead to growing to do great things with our lives. By counteracting what could have caused pain or damaged in one form or the other, you instead achieve growth. When you make a choice that leads to the realisation that you have done the right thing, you experience a sense of accomplishment, feel freer and even be eager to do more.

Drifting through life without clear understanding of what you can really do, why you are able to do what you do and not others, and most importantly where you are going makes you live apprehensively not knowing what is going to happen next and what you can make happen. Own your life. Let the real you come forth and take charge. Knowing who you really are, allowing yourself to grow by doing better than you previous best, adopting a winning attitude will indeed help you achieve personal excellence. Since you can never reach the end of what you can be, this is a lifetime project. Embark on this long journey by learning what is really important for you, spend your time where it matters and will benefit you most. Thus you take control of your life.

> ==> Be the expert about you – know who you really are.
> ==> Take responsibility for your life and direct it to be what you want it to be.
> ==> Master your emotions and make them work for you.

Personal Checklist

1. Are my people skills developed enough to allow me to effectively get the best out of everyone?
2. How secure am I in my skills to effectively draw from them to do my work well?
3. Am I ready to take up opportunities as they arise to do my personal best?
4. Is my attitude towards collaborating with others clear to allow me to help everyone succeed in our projects?
5. Am I able to communicate effectively with others?
6. Do I need to take steps to sharpen my communication skills?
7. Have I put in place a working system that enables me to never stop growing

When you have worked hard to achieve a state of being, you will not be satisfied to stay there. An attitude of continued growth demands even more of yourself, such that you seek to give quality output and, serve better at all times. As you surmount one peak, another appears. You will always realise as you travel the difficult route to the top, that you never really get there. On reaching what you thought was the very top, another peak always appears in the horizon. No matter how far to the top you go, there is still more to learn, to conquer, to achieve. You just have to keep scratching. There is nothing like a simple, single answer to fulfilling one's desires. For in searching for the essence of anything, you find yourself opening up a whole lot more avenues hitherto unknown, thus you get to learn even more. With each successful step forward you get closer and closer to the essence of that which you seek. Yet complete fulfilment always eludes you. Your satisfaction should come from knowing that you are perpetually in search of personal excellence.

Success for you will then remain giving your best at all times. And this you will do best when:
- √ you understand yourself, taking advantage of your strengths;
- √ acquiring useful habits;
- √ serving others well;
- √ working well as a team member;
- √ knowing what to say and saying it effectively;
- √ doing what has to be done efficiently and being effective, i.e. producing quality per unit time.

Own your life - be the best you can ever be.

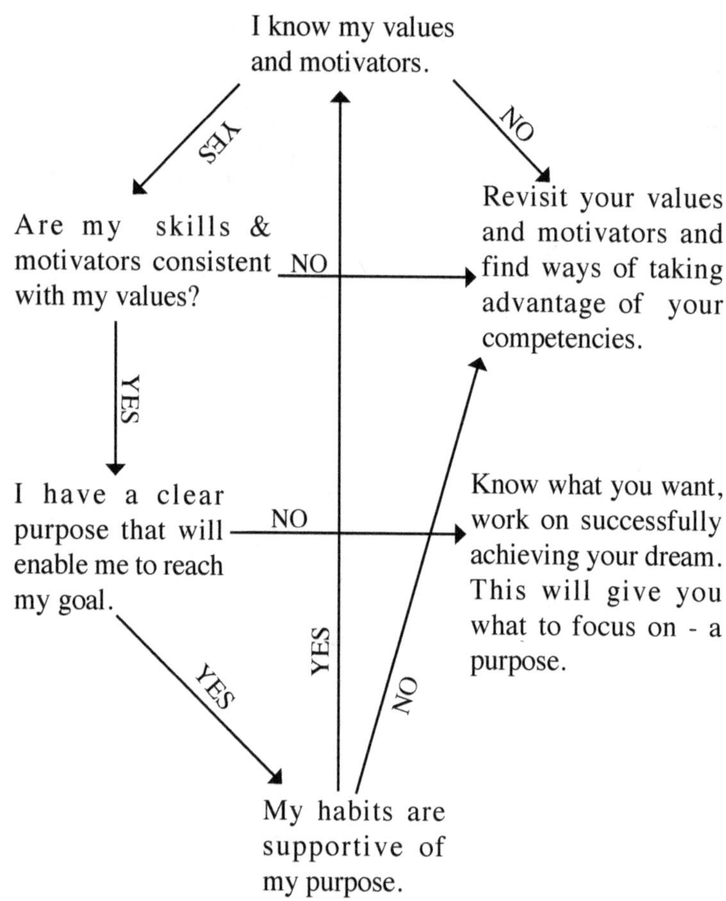

I know my values and motivators.
YES
NO
Are my skills & motivators consistent with my values?
Revisit your values and motivators and find ways of taking advantage of your competencies.
NO
YES
I have a clear purpose that will enable me to reach my goal.
NO
Know what you want, work on successfully achieving your dream. This will give you what to focus on - a purpose.
YES
YES
NO
My habits are supportive of my purpose.

Also by Keleapere Maggie Chalebgwa

The Journey to Discover Your True Self   ISBN: 978-99912-940-1-8

123

www.ingramcontent.com/pod-product-compliance
Lightning Source LLC
Chambersburg PA
CBHW050535160726
48003CB00002B/604